Materials and Craft of the Scenic Model

Darwin Reid Payne

With 81 illustrations

Southern Illinois University Press · *Carbondale and Edwardsville*

Feffer & Simons, Inc. · *London and Amsterdam*

For Norman Young

Library of Congress Cataloging in Publication Data

Payne, Darwin Reid.
    Materials and craft of the scenic model.

    Bibliography: p.
    Includes index.
    1. Theaters—Models.   I. Title.
PN2091.M6P37   792′.025′0228   76-15230
ISBN 0-8093-0778-2
ISBN 0-8093-0783-9 pbk.

Designed by Gary Gore

Contents

List of Figures

Acknowledgments

Much of the material in this book deals with the visual and can be presented and understood only visually. I would like, therefore, to take this opportunity to express my gratitude to Elliott Mendelson for his great care in recording that material with skill and clarity. And I think all who read this book will be grateful to him for his thoughts (as well as the example of his own work) concerning the many problems both the designer and photographer encounter when trying to capture the three-dimensional spirit of the scenic model in the photographic image.

Introduction

This book is the second in a series of texts dealing with the art and craft of stage design. The earlier work, *Design for the Stage: First Steps,* dealt only with the conceptual basis of the designer's art; there the student was introduced to many of the principles and differing philosophies which underlie and inform the practice of scene design. The present work, however, broaches few philosophic or aesthetic matters; nor does it deal with the entire field of scenic craftsmanship. Its primary purpose is, rather, to discuss and demonstrate to beginning students of scene design the craft and techniques involved in preparing one of the designer's most helpful presentations, the scenic model. But although this book is limited to only one aspect of the designer's work, the tacit assumption will be that the principles of the first book have been studied and absorbed and that the artistic directions suggested here will actively inform and further all the techniques and skills the designer needs in the practice of his profession. Most importantly, he must constantly keep in mind that when art and craftsmanship are separated, not much remains of either one. And while other areas of scenic craftsmanship are barely touched upon in this book, the need for their mastery by the student is patently assumed. It will not take long for the serious student to discover, however, that while texts can be helpful in his education, they are only useful to the extent that they promote an active desire to work and experiment outside and beyond the guidelines set down here.

The making of scale scenic models is certainly not a new development in the theater. The scenic model has been in existence as long as scenery itself; Leonardo da Vinci made scale working models for the elaborate machines which figured importantly in the spectacles he was commissioned to design. In Shakespeare's time, the Revels Office provided paper models ("in the Italian style," reads a contemporary account) to the artisans who built and painted scenery for the court masques. In fact, every period of theater history from the late Renaissance on has produced, with many examples still extant, scenic models as a regular feature of production practice. It has only been during the past few decades, however, that the making of the model has all but superseded the making of scenic sketches. There are many reasons for this new emphasis, but perhaps the most important one is that the designers working in today's theater realize that the art they practice is becoming less and less that of the painter and more a matter of space and three-dimensional form. Very often the scenic sketch cannot show what the present-day designer intends. The whole trend of twentieth-century scene design has been, in fact, away from flats and painted drops and toward a stronger feeling for sculptural form. A host of new materials and construction techniques has made this trend both possible and economical; the old supremacy of illusory scene painting as the dominate feature of scenic design has been successfully challenged. Add to this the ever-increasing use of kinetic scenery and the almost infinite possibilities which light and projection provide, and it is easy to understand why the single pictorial image has become less and less useful as a means of demonstrating what the designer can do on the stage. For these reasons, the scenic model can often better show these newer trends and developments. In short, the scenic model has come into its own. There are, however, other very practical reasons why the student of design should master the skills needed to make these structures. Briefly, a few of these could be listed thus:

1. Scenic-model making is a more comprehendible skill for the beginning student to develop than that of illusory painting. This is not to suggest that drawing and painting are not necessary skills for the scene designer; indeed, their mastery is absolutely essential to him. If, however, the student designer begins directly with those elements which more nearly touch the basic nature of his art—three-dimensional form, texture, space, and the effect of light on these elements—his progress is apt to be more rapid in other areas of visual art. Model making can, in fact, serve as a focus for pursuing more graphic skills; drawing from the scenic model, in fact, can greatly enhance the student's appreciation of the particular kind of space with which he must deal.

2. The scenic model provides an image nearer to what can be realized on the actual stage than does the set sketch. Moreover, unlike a set sketch, this image can be quickly viewed from more than one vantage point. Figure 1 shows a scenic drawing. It does have certain advantages; the nature of graphic materials allows the designer to make this work more atmospheric than most models can be. A sketch can also indicate precise lighting effects; this aspect of a scenic drawing can be very helpful in either working out a desired lighting plot or indicating to a light designer (or clarify for himself, if the designer is lighting his own production) a desired mood. Yet we are still limited to this one view; and that view is totally incapable of giving a true approximation of the three-dimensional space in which the actual setting will exist. Figure 2 is a scenic model of the same design. In some ways it is less "artful" than the sketch; the model is by necessity more solid and, if you will, more crude. It is certainly less atmospheric. Nevertheless, this model does allow us to see what will really exist on the stage, what we can realistically expect to accomplish as a designer, and what we can lead others to expect from our work. In the long run, the scenic model deludes us less about what is possible in the the-

1. *Scenic sketch:* The Effect of Gamma Rays on Man-In-The-Moon Marigolds

2. *Scenic model:* The Effect
of Gamma Rays on Man-
In-The-Moon Marigolds

3. *Floor-line view of model*

4. *Side view of model*

ater. We can, in fact, view the model in any number of ways not possible with the single set sketch alone (Figs. *3, 4, 5*). Scenic models automatically force the designer to approach his design from the outset as a real structure which must be seen from virtually hundreds of vantage points, not as a picture viewed from one static point.

3. The model inherently provides more hard information for the various shops and technicians whose responsibility it is to build the actual setting. Not only does a model show how a particular scenic unit will appear on the stage, it can also reveal the assembly of all individual units into the complete setting. Moreover, in the multiscene production, it allows both the stage manager and technical director to plan and provide for the flow of traffic of the component parts of the setting from scene change to scene change. A model also allows the designer to check more accurately the effect he intends against the limitations of the physical stage; set sketches, with their easily achieved atmospheric effects and limitless possibility of form, tend to lull the designer into a false sense of what can be done in the real world of production. Of course, imagination should never be prematurely thwarted; but if the designer is not artistically equipped to deliver on

5. *Top view of model*

the stage what he shows in his preliminary designs, he had best work in some other field of art.

4. While precise lighting effects are difficult to obtain with a scenic model, it does allow the designer (or independent lighting designer if the scenic designer does not light the production himself) to better plan for the placement of lighting instruments in order to gain desired effects. The designer can, however, show the lighting designer precisely the areas and angles where light is necessary to best realize the visual effects originally intended.

5. A model gives the director a much clearer view of how his own work will relate to the production as a whole. It will also show very quickly any problems he might have with the design, problems which might not be readily apparent in a scenic sketch; spatial relationships are much more easily seen on the model than on a flat floor plan or in a drawing of a setting. This is, perhaps, the most important reason for making a model; much misunderstanding can be prevented by the use of a carefully scaled model.

6. Models often take more time to make than set sketches; this can be a decided advantage to the designer. Quite often a designer's initial concept, expressed in quickly drawn sketches, is modified, deepened and refined precisely because of the longer work period required in model making. It is not uncommon, in fact, for the designer to change the whole form of a setting drastically without changing the basic idea behind it, and in so doing improve his contribution to the total production. These changes are often better illustrated by the use of models than by set sketches. In any case, they show the real changes in form, scale, and placement more accurately than drawings (Figs. 6 and 7). A beautiful set drawing, it must be admitted, can be a powerful inducement for a director to accept a designer's early idea; like the printed word, the well-defined image carries great authority. But it should also be kept in mind that getting one's way

too soon is often more disastrous than not getting it at all.

Of course, different designers have differing views as to what the model should do and what techniques should be employed in making them. Most certainly, as the designer progresses in his career, the suggestions presented here will be modified, changed, and perhaps abandoned. That is only natural in the maturation of any artist. Nevertheless, it is hoped the information presented here will be of some value. If nothing else, it should provide those new to the craft of model building with a good point of departure, and beginnings are important in any field of endeavor. The most important point to remember about perfecting any craft, however, is that all the steps which go into it must be thoroughly understood conceptually as well as assimilated manually; skill is simply the hand doing what the mind tells it; accuracy, while it depends much upon practice, is also a state of mind. On the other hand, important as inspiration or a natural grasp of artistic problems is to the artist, he must also know how to build his product in much the same way as the cabinetmaker creates a piece of furniture or a baker makes a cake. Mastery of his craft cannot, unfortunately, assure the student a secure place in his profession; without it, however, he won't get many opportunities to try for the recognition all artists want.

Perhaps one note of caution would not be out of

6. *Scenic model:* Suddenly Last Summer

7. *Scenic model: Alternate variation of* Suddenly Last Summer

place at this point. It touches on something which will always remain true for the designer using models in his work. Although not the only person to warn about the limitations of the scenic model in the theater, Jean Cocteau has, perhaps, stated it more concisely than almost anyone else: "To reproduce a model too precisely on a stage is one of the greatest faults in theatrical craftsmanship." What he means, simply, is that it is a mistake not to recognize that relationships change—often drastically—as scales change, and that the designer must always keep his critical eye open to what those changes are and how they must be dealt with. He also meant that the model is only a step in the theatrical design process not, as some scenic sketches do become, an artistic end in itself. As helpful as the model setting is—and it does have much to recommend it—it also has its own particular artistic dangers.

Darwin Reid Payne

Carbondale, Illinois
November 1975

Part 1 *Basic Preparation*

1. Tools and Materials

Since we are most concerned in this book with demonstrating the mechanical skills and techniques the designer needs in model making, it should be kept in mind that the mastery of these skills will always be greatly influenced by the tools and materials used. If they are inferior, outstanding results cannot be achieved; if they are well made and of quality, they will actively aid the designer in his development. Still, it is not necessarily true that the most expensive item is the best; nor is every tool available for model making necessary. Few designers need all the tools listed in the various catalogues put out by manufacturers of drafting and model making equipment. Those needed most are few and relatively inexpensive—especially if viewed as long-term investments. In fact, most of the designer's basic equipment will be serviceable for many years if given a modicum of care. But if the designer tries to "make do" with inferior tools and materials, such as the watercolor sets sold in the toy departments of inexpensive chain stores, or attempts to paint with a fifteen-cent brush on newsprint, he should not expect professional results from his efforts. In any case, he won't get them. For these reasons, recommendations as to specific types of tools and materials will be suggested. Of course, it is to be expected that as each designer progresses in his career, he will develop affinities for certain kinds of tools and materials not included in the following pages. They may, in fact, totally contradict the recommendations made there. But the principle remains true for any item eventually replacing those suggested in this book: good tools conscientiously maintained and quality materials carefully selected can go far in helping the designer to use his time most effectively and insure for him the best possible transfer of his concepts into practical stage realities.

Basic Tools for Model Construction

Drawing Tools (Not Shown)

T square (at least 24 inches)
Triangles (30°–60° and 45°)
Architect scale (a flat scale with ¼ inch equals 1 foot and ½ inch equals 1 foot is a handier tool than the usual architect's scale)
Mechanical pencil and sharpener
Compass (with an extension arm for making larger circles)
French curve or flexible curve maker

Model Construction Tools (Figure 8)

a. X-acto knife (slim barrel for No. 11 blade)
b. Razor saw (blades are interchangeable)

1

8. *Model construction tools*

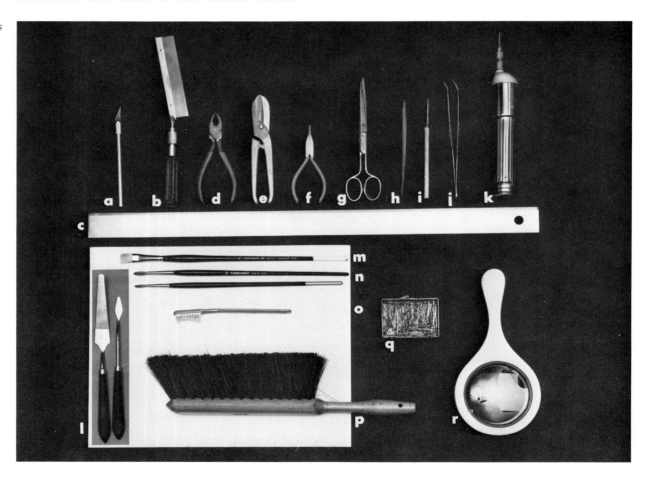

c. Steel edge (at least 18 inches) for guiding cutting edges
d. Small wire cutters
e. Small tin snips
f. Needle-nose pliers
g. Scissors
h. Small rat-tail file
i. Biology probe (for making small holes and holding pieces together while applying glue)
j. Biology tweezers (for handling small pieces)
k. Small battery-powered drill (with interchangeable bits)
l. Painting knives (for application and working of modeling paste)
m. Gesso brush (for application of gesso)
n. Sable watercolor brushes (for painting detail on exhibition models)
o. Toothbrush (for spattering paint effects on exhibition models)
p. Architect's cleaning brush (a necessity for keeping the model making space clean of waste materials)
q. Large dressmaker's pins (The larger the head, the easier the pin is to use and the easier on the fingertips. These pins do not bend as readily as lighter ones.)
r. Reducing glass (The opposite of a magnifying glass; it allows a work to be seen in a smaller dimension but with increased sharpness. Thus the larger outlines of the work are better revealed while the details are reduced to a more subordinate proportion. This tool also aids the designer when making set sketches to get a fresh perspective on his work.)

Materials for Model Construction (Figure 9)

a. Various paper boards, thinner papers, foils, and textiles
b. Balsa woods of various sizes
c. Styrofoam pieces
d. Wire screening and meshes of various weaves
e. Wire, metal pieces, and plates
f. Found objects (twigs, chain, rusted metal pieces, prefabricated forms, etc.)
g. Found images

NOTE: Hobby and art supply stores carry balsa woods and traditional model-making supplies. Recently they have also begun to stock small metal rods and pipes of various dimensions as. well as metal plates; these can be obtained in several types of metal—brass, aluminum, chrome-plate, etc. Wire screening and meshes are obtainable at building supply or hardware stores.

9. *Materials for model construction*

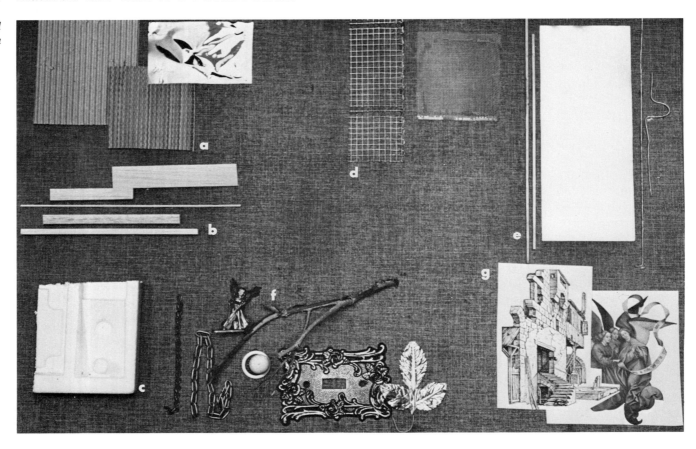

*Materials for Assembly and Finishing
Models (Not Shown)*

a. Gesso
b. Modeling paste
c. Plastic sand (available from paint supply stores)
d. Masking tape
e. Duco cement (recommended above all others)
f. Rubber cement
g. Elmer's glue (the best of the white glues)
h. Inks (sepia and black)
i. Tempera paints (all basic colors)
j. Water-soluble metallic colors (This is a relatively new product and comes in a variety of finishes: gold, silver, copper, brass, etc. Regular metallic paints are not recommended for use on exhibition models except, in some instances, metallic sprays.)
k. Tube watercolors (for more transparent painted effects on exhibition models)
l. Metallic paste (This is a product that is not water-soluble. These finishes—gold, silver, copper, brass—can be used to enrich and add highlights to the textured surfaces of an exhibition model. See part 2, section 7, under Finishing the Exhibition Model.)
m. Various aerosol spray paints, stains, and sealers

NOTE: An airbrush is a helpful, although rather expensive, tool. It allows the designer to substitute water-soluble paints for painting basic coats on the model. It is also a more refined method of obtaining shaded effects than possible with aerosol spray products.

2. The Designer's Work Space

Doubtless no two designers could be expected to have identical work patterns; the individual manner in which each designer works, therefore, probably accounts more for the great variation one encounters from studio to studio than architectural differences. Nevertheless most studios of scene designers could be expected to have certain features in common.

Practically all artists find that the place they work has a definite effect on the kind of work they do; partly in the amount they are able to produce and also in the quality of that work. And the deeper they become involved in their profession, the more particular they are about not only the tools and materials of their craft but where they employ them. To the working designer, organization of his work area is not a restrictive activity, it is one that allows him to advance most freely. But what are some of the work needs of the designer? How are they expressed in work areas? Some of these needs one would almost certainly encounter in most studios would be:

1. A place to think, make rough sketches, confer with others concerned with the production.

2. A place to make finished sketches: watercolor, pastel, pen and ink, etc. (with a water supply near this area if possible).

3. A place to create and experiment with models and to be able to work with three-dimensional materials.

4. A place to make large-sheet working drawings (a drafting table).

5. Storage areas for: reference books (shelving); file clippings, catalogues, etc. (file cabinets); working drawings (flat files); sketches and set drawings (flat files or racks); drawing materials, drafting supplies, model materials (shelving, chests); finished models (shelving); slides and projections (slide files).

6. Display areas for current ideas, notes, schedules, etc., near working areas (bulletin boards).

7. A projection screen on which to show slides and a permanent setup for projector.

8. An all-purpose worktable on which to lay out work in progress, draw up full-scale details, etc.

(All these areas should have general lighting [from the studio's overall illumination] but should also have specifically directed light sources in each individual area.)

9. And, although not an absolute necessity, provision for refreshment—an area for coffee-making, etc.—and marginal entertainment: phonograph, radio. A designer spends a great deal of time in his studio; although it is a working place, it should be as comfortable as he can make it.

After only a few years, most designers find they need additional storage space for past projects (or for materials they might not need to use very often). The working designer, therefore, should examine his studio from time to time and store in some other place all the things he does not absolutely need. Nothing is quite as exasperating as trying to put together a complicated production and having its component parts constantly being lost in a welter of past projects or unimportant materials. Few professional designers can afford the luxury of being unorganized. Figure *10* is a drawing that incorporates these work necessities into a workable studio layout:

A. Study and conference area

B. Storage for drafting materials and art supplies

C. Drafting table—immediate reference materials and supplies kept in shelving above

D. Bulletin board

E. Sketching and model building area

F. Storage shelving for models

G. File cabinets

H. Flat file cabinets

I. Projection screen (pulls down when used)
J. Book shelving
K. All-purpose worktable
L. Slide storage
M. Slide projector

Model making almost invariably requires more work space than that for rendering scenic sketches or making working drawings. Also, the number of materials and tools is greater and requires more ample storage space. While a single working area can be used for almost all the projects a designer needs to make, if at all possible, keep areas which have different working requirements separate. For instance, the drafting area should never be used for any great amount of cutting or painting; the surface of the table needed for making accurate working drawings will become permanently damaged very quickly if used in such a way. In fact, the work area for model making takes a great deal of punishment and should have a surface impervious to the materials and tools which could render a drafting table unusable. Figure 11 shows the specific area a model maker might arrange in the studio for an efficient work pattern. As with other parts of the studio, lighting is extremely important; more than one source is required with the brightest amount of light coming from in front of the area where detailed work is to be done. The shadowless light of fluorescent fixtures is especially helpful in model

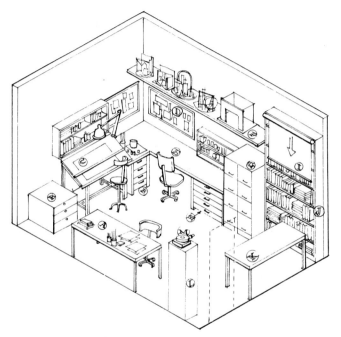

10. *The designer's work space*

11. *Scenic-model building
area*

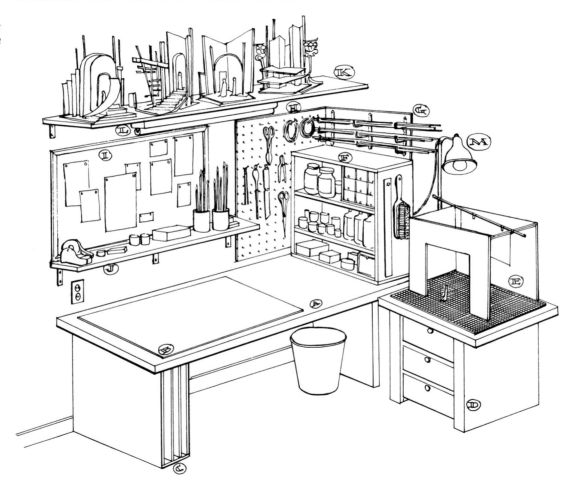

making; making accurate cuts in materials such as illustration board is difficult if hard shadows are cast by the cutting guide.

A. Basic work area: this surface should be covered with a strong material such as formica which resists scarring and can be easily cleaned of materials accidentally spilled on it.

B. Removable working board: even though the general work table is constructed to withstand hard usage, an expendable material should be used for cutting, gluing, and texturing model parts. One-half-inch plywood, untempered masonite, or heavy illustration board is suitable and makes it economically feasible to change this surface at regular intervals.

C. Vertical storage of flat materials: illustration board, bristol board, acetate, etc.

D. Storage for basic supplies of materials not needed for immediate use.

E. The model stage (see part 2, section 5, for details of construction): this unit should be kept in close proximity to the working area so that model pieces can be quickly tested for size, scale, and placement.

F. Shelf storage for materials constantly in use: gesso, modeling paste, paint, pins, adhesives, etc.

G. Racks for balsa materials: display of these materials not only keeps them unbroken and available, it also keeps the designer aware of what is in short supply.

H. Pegboard for tools constantly in use: nothing is as exasperating as looking for a specific tool and not being able to locate it. This type of display unit makes it easy to find a tool and then gives a place to return it when no longer needed.

I. Bulletin board: a designer simply cannot function properly without an ample area on which to display all the notes and images that remind him of the various facets of the projects being worked upon.

J. A shelf immediately above the working area helps keep small items and materials out of the way or from being misplaced. Model making often requires a number of processes being worked upon at the same time, usually involving a large number of materials and tools. Great frustration can be avoided by keeping the immediate working area orderly.

K. The best place to keep completed models is on shelving up and out of the immediate working area of the studio. It does help to have them, however, within close range for reference.

L. General lighting fixture above and in front of the work area: warm-toned fluorescent light is probably best for this purpose because it is virtually shadowless and does not glare.

M. A small incandescent lamp above the model stage unit is useful not only for its illumination, but also because it makes possible the viewing of the model under the effect of directed light. Although, at best, this use of light can give only crude approximations, the information it imparts can be helpful.

3. Types of Scenic Models

The Experimental Model

The experimental model is not so much a type of model as it is an activity (Fig. *12*). Often the designer will begin to search for a design concept with three-dimensional forms and materials directly on a scaled model stage. He does not, when working in this manner, first draw out a predetermined design and then build a scale replica of it. Rather, he usually cuts out and assembles materials and objects with little regard as to measurement or scale. The object of this activity is, as its name implies, to determine scenic ideas in an experimental way rather than thinking them out beforehand conceptually or on paper. This activity is meant to begin the creative process in a more direct manner than sketching would allow; it also relies heavily on the designer's intuitive ability to see possibilities in accidental results. It is, in fact, nothing much more than creative play—but with an eventual purpose. It is possible for the designer to create accidental and random arrangements which could lead to solution when, in the formative stages of a design concept,

he finds himself at an impasse. A variety of materials can be used in this experimental model—wire mesh and screening, metal foils, plastics, modeling clay, photographic images, fabrics, string, Styrofoam, etc.—as well as the traditional cardboard, heavy paper, and balsa wood. The designer should also keep in mind that in the present-day theater practically any form or texture used in these models can be duplicated in full scale on the stage in any number of lightweight materials and so he should not be afraid of being "impractical" in his choice of exotic forms or materials. It is advisable, however, that the human scale always be present in these models (as, indeed, with all scenic models); this is easily remembered if a scale figure is constantly kept on the model stage.

The Working Model

The working model's primary function is to show how the exact form of the setting will appear on stage. It is usually evolved from experimental model possibilities. The working model, however, must be as accurate in detail as possible. This model is almost always finished with a coat of gesso so that the various materials used—balsa, illustration board, wire, etc.—will have a common tonality and surface finish; this makes it easier to see the total form of the setting without the distraction of differing materials (Fig. *13*).

13. *A working model:*
Arsenic and Old Lace

Occasionally, designers may draft onto the working model architectural details in pencil or ink; this is a common practice in making the lightweight bristol board model. It is also a common practice to construct the working model in the actual units which will be used in the full-scale setting (Fig. *14*).

This approach not only helps the shops to study the construction requirements of the individual units, it also helps to understand how they will be assembled, separated, and stored when the setting is actually in the theater. The working model is more a tool than something to be shown as a work of art; often they do not survive their usefulness in the scenic shops.

The Exhibition Model

The exhibition model (Fig. *15*), unlike the working model, is completely finished; that is, it is painted as nearly as possible to show the color and treatment of the scenic units as they are to appear on the stage. As its name suggests, it is purposefully made to be shown and, like scenic sketches, often assumes an artistic value beyond its usefulness as working information for scenic technicians. While the working model is usually made to come apart so that the shifting routine of the actual setting can be studied, the exhibition model is often (but not always) built as a solid unit. Often a designer will not take the time to complete a model such as this; it does require considerably more time while adding little more information than that given by the working model. Nevertheless, if the designer is interested in "selling" a particular idea or wants to make quite sure those working on the actual setting understand just how he wants the final product to appear, nothing is quite as persuasive as this type of model.

NOTE: Part 2, section 7 (see Finishing the Exhibition Model), discusses additional techniques and materials necessary for this type of model.

14. *A working model (in component parts)*

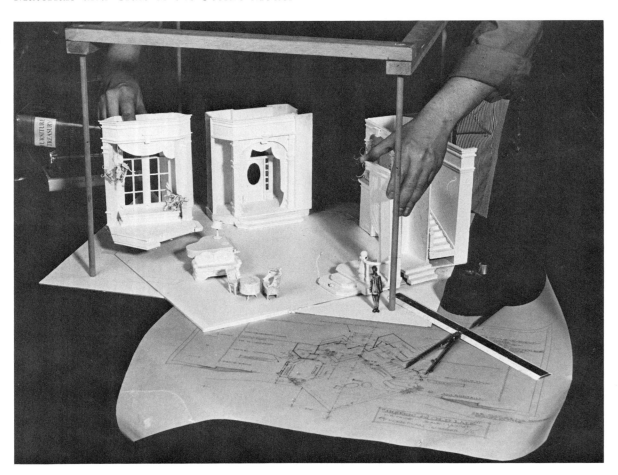

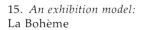

15. *An exhibition model:*
La Bohème

Part 2 *The Craft of Scenic-Model Making*

4. The Basic Phases

While it is not probable that all designers will follow exactly the same steps in planning a production, the process of making the scenic model does by necessity have a certain fundamental line of development. The two most basic phases of this process are as follows:

The Conceptual Stage

All models start as an idea, a concept without physical form. There are, however, several initial options which the designer may choose when he is ready to put his idea into material terms. He may, before any three-dimensional work is begun, sketch out a diagram or picture of what he intends to make. On the other hand, he may decide to begin directly with three-dimensional materials without any prior graphic work. In all probability, he will, in the earliest stages of developing his idea, need to do a great deal of both. By that we mean that rarely is any art work a straight-line activity with clearly defined steps, one following the other. Model making, like all other artwork, tends to proceed in a leapfrog fashion; a sketch may precede an actual form, but it is also possible that a form or a configuration of forms arrived at experimentally on the small model stage will then be recorded in a sketch. This sketch might, in turn, suggest further possibil-ities, and so on until a viable solution is reached. The designer will find, in fact, that as he works on project after project it becomes increasingly difficult to separate graphic work from three-dimensional experimentation; in any case, the professional designer should be expert in both areas.

The Construction of the Final Model

Once definite ideas are formulated, a number of operations must be performed. These are:

1. Drafting of the floor plan onto a base plane. Usually this base is the heaviest material—or as heavy as any material—in the model. One-hundred-weight cold press illustration board is probably the best material for this base regardless of the type of model being made. Anything of less substance will usually warp; if this happens, nothing placed on it will stand straight. Heavier materials, such as ply-wood or masonite, are overkill; also their surfaces do not respond to art materials such as watercolor, tempera, or inks as well as illustration board.

2. Drafting the component parts of the model. This is done by the same techniques and procedures employed in making regular front elevations for working drawings. The only difference is the draft-ing is done on whatever material will be used in the model; the weight in large part determines the type of model being made.

3. Cutting and assembly of the parts into scenic

units. For working models, these units will correspond directly to the units made in the scenic shop.

4. Application of textures and three-dimensional detail to the basic units. Paper models will have this detail indicated by graphic means; more finished models and exhibition models will require other materials for their completion: gesso, modeling paste, glued-on textures, etc.

5. Final finish of the model. For the paper model, graphic work completes it; for the working model, the gesso coat is the last step; for the exhibition model, a number of steps follow the gesso coating— painting, shading, highlighting are all necessary for this model, as well as detailed set dressing and scale representations of the performer.

(Below, we will be examining in greater detail all the steps encompassed in these two phases of model making. But, before proceeding directly to the specific techniques of model building, let us examine a very important piece of equipment necessary to the whole craft of scenic models: the model stage unit.

5. The Model Stage Unit: Its Construction and Use

It is taken for granted that all designers need an ability to sketch an idea on paper quickly. These drawings, often crude and sketchy, are usually diagrammatic and reveal only the most basic form of the intended design. Many professional designers will even admit that they make their exhibition drawings after the actual design has been realized on the stage. These designers frankly state they do not have time to make detailed set drawings before that time. What then does take precedent over elaborate renderings? In many instances experimentation on the model stage is the answer. In fact, it is not uncommon for the designer to begin almost directly with three-dimensional work although, as we have said, almost all do commit their very first thoughts to paper in small, quickly drawn diagrams. Figure *16* shows such a unit with a model being constructed within its boundaries.

For many designers this approach is more productive than a strictly pictorial one. And while it might be thought that the model is a product which has been completely worked out on paper before its construction, such is rarely the case. The real value of the model stage unit lies in the opportunities it affords the designer to test ideas before giving the scenic model its final form. In fact, the designer who uses the model stage often does not begin making working drawings or final set sketches until after he has satisfied himself with the shape and form of the set he has worked out experimentally on this stage.

This unit, therefore, to be of any real value, must

be constructed as a type of instrument which can immediately reveal the placement of objects and structural units quickly and accurately in a known scale. The floor of such a unit should be a grid system which allows for an immediate reading of anything placed on it. Figure 17 is a diagram of a model stage unit in its simplest form.

It is not difficult or expensive to build a unit similar to the one shown; even with hand-tools, it can be constructed fairly quickly using the diagram given here as a guideline. While basically a simple structure, other features found on the actual full-scale stage can be included: line-sets noted both on the floor and on the top side-bars, removable traps, masking, etc. Most professional designers have a unit similar to this (some more complicated than others) in their studios and make constant use of it in their work. In Richard Pilbrow's book, *Stage Lighting,* page 49 contains a model stage unit complete with fly loft and counterweights as well as a working electrical system. Few designers need (or could afford) such a setup. In fact, Jo Mielziner, who had just such a model stage in the 1930s, candidly admitted sometime later that precise lighting problems simply could not be worked out on this type of unit with any degree of accuracy, that his own stage was not much more than a rather elaborate toy which, although a great deal of fun, produced definitely limited results. While the unit recommended

here is elemental, it will provide the designer with good workable information, actively suggesting configurations and alternatives he would never discover with only pen or pencil.

While objects placed on the floor grid can be immediately read in terms of size and placement at ground level, those images or objects which exist above the floor level are not as easily put into an accurate context. There is a device, however, which will allow the designer to place a number of images into various relationships—both to the model stage structure as well as to each other—which can be accurately measured. The device is simple and consists of two basic parts. One part consists of a number of clear acetate "drops." These are nothing more than pieces of acetate approximately 15 by 15 inches with a small dowel rod taped to one edge which allows them to hang vertically from the top bars of the model stage down to the stage floor. The other part is a piece of illustration board, also approximately 15 by 15 inches, which, like the acetate sheets, has a dowel rod attached to one edge. It, however, is a grid similar to the stage floor and in the same scale. To use these two parts, simply tape any selected image or images onto the acetate sheets in whatever pattern is desired and hang from the crossbars over the floor grid. When the desired visual effect is obtained, drop the grid piece behind the acetate one; placement of the image can then be

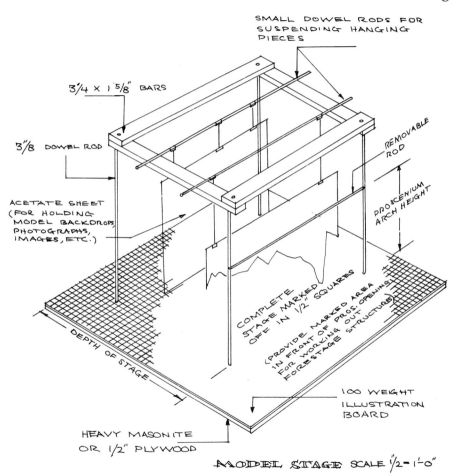

SMALL DOWEL RODS FOR
SUSPENDING HANGING
PIECES

17. *Diagram of model stage unit*

3¼ × 1⅝" BARS

3/8" DOWEL ROD

REMOVABLE ROD

ACETATE SHEET
(FOR HOLDING
MODEL BACKDROPS,
PHOTOGRAPHS,
IMAGES, ETC.)

PROSCENIUM ARCH HEIGHT

COMPLETE
STAGE MARKED
OFF IN ½" SQUARES

(PROVIDE MARKED AREA
IN FRONT OF PROS. OPENING
FOR WORKING OUT
FORESTAGE STRUCTURE)

DEPTH OF STAGE

100 WEIGHT
ILLUSTRATION
BOARD

HEAVY MASONITE
OR ½" PLYWOOD

MODEL STAGE SCALE ½"–1'–0"

read in scale. Precise measurements are obtainable in this manner as to the image's height from the floor plane; its distance from center line and from curtain line can be read by noting where the vertical grid touches the floor grid. Figure *18* should clear up any questions concerning the use of this helpful adjunct to the model stage structure. In Figure *19*, the treetop forms are secured to acetate drops similar to the ones just described.

NOTE: See part 3, section 9, for additional discussion of found images for use in the scenic model.

6. Recording Initial Ideas

Drawing and Quick Sketches

While it is not possible to detail a complete step-by-step outline of the designer's work pattern in model making, there are certain features of this pattern which could be expected to be similar for most designers and the first of these steps most probably would be some form of graphic note making.

All designers must be able to draw. Most designers, in fact, cannot think without pen or pencil. Almost all certainly precede even the crudest three-dimensional structure with graphic work of some sort. Usually these drawings are not meant for the eyes of any but the designer himself; they are noth-

ing much more than a visual shorthand which he alone can later interpret. The character and number of these drawings, moreover, vary greatly with individual designers. Therefore, in the very first encounters with an idea, the designer needs materials and techniques which will allow him to record his idea in the most expeditious manner. Over a period of time, most designers develop strong affinities for those tools and methods which allow him to express his ideas in the most immediate way. It should always be kept in mind that drawing has distinctly different purposes at the various stages of the design process.

At a later time the designer will probably make more elaborate set sketches to supplement the model. For now, however, we are concerned only with the very first drawings the designer makes—the initial idea expressed in its most elemental form—and then only as a step toward the construction of a scenic model. The tools and materials for this work are relatively simple and inexpensive:

1. Pencils. While most designers prefer H leads (2H, 3H, for example) for drafting, B leads, which are softer and darker, are better suited for sketching. Colored pencils can at times suggest qualities not possible with black lead alone.

2. Pen and ink. The various mechanical pens now available which use India ink, such as Rapidiograph, are favorite sketching tools for many de-

18. *Model stage unit with acetate drops*

19. *Scenic model:* As You
Like It

signers. Since the points are numbered and interchangeable, a designer can select the quality of line that best suits his needs or temperament. The simple inexpensive crow-quill pen also retains a certain amount of popularity.

3. The felt-tip pen. This type of pen has become a very popular tool for designers. Its relatively low cost plus the range of colors and tips available make it an attractive tool for sketching. Another advantage it possesses is the receptiveness of most felt-tip lines to brush and water: a line drawing such as the one shown in Figure 20 can, when water is applied, become a quick, monochromatic watercolor sketch with atmospheric qualities not found in line drawings (Fig. 21).

It should be kept in mind, however, that drawings which are diagrammatic in nature are of more value to the designer whose intent is to make a three-dimensional structure. These drawings, unlike most scenic sketches, stress the placement of solid forms in space rather than the flat pictorial qualities of the finished set drawing. Figure 22, therefore, with its higher vanishing point, shows a truer approximation of the setting's depth; this type of drawing better serves the designer than Figure 23, which does not show much floor space at all.

In fact, a drawing such as the isometric sketch shown in Figure 24, which shows no perspective at all, is probably more useful as a step in the model making process than those drawings which are more concerned with pictorial compositional values. Here real space is easier to see and comprehend than in any sketch in perspective. It would be well to keep in mind Adolphe Appia's advice to a student of design to "design with your legs, not with your eyes."

4. Conte crayon. The Conte crayon—both black and red—has long been a favorite sketching tool for designers: Its value, however, lies in its ability to give atmospheric qualities—the play of light and shadow—quickly. It is less useful to the designer whose primary purpose is determining the constituent forms of a model.

5. Layout pad. Usually a sketch goes through a series of modifications; the nature of the layout paper is that, unlike tracing paper, it has body enough to withstand pen and ink or a limited amount of watercolor but, unlike most other types of paper, is transparent enough to make tracing of images feasible.

Preliminary Paper Structures

Quite often preliminary three-dimensional work and rough sketching go hand in hand. And, while it is not uncommon for a designer to begin exploration of a possibility directly on the model stage—manipulating forms and materials in a creatively

20. *Felt-tip drawing*

21. *Felt-tip drawing (after water application)*

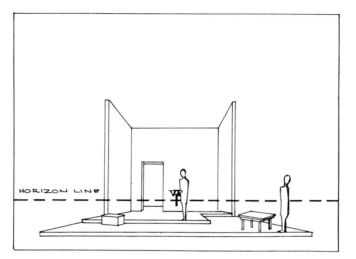

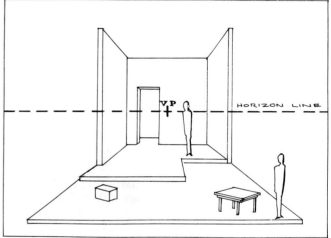

undirected form of play—almost all do make rough drawings of an idea or of an isolated unit of scenery beforehand. Most often the process follows a line of development such as the one indicated in Figure 25.

Here the sketch (Fig. *25a*) helps determine a basic intention. This drawing is less useful, however, than the crude paper structure which is made after it, which, incidentally, has drawing on it to indicate features which in the final structure will be three-dimensional (Fig. *25b*). While the final unit (Fig. *25c*) certainly had its inception in the sketch, it was

the paper structure which allowed the designer to make the real decisions as to its scale, size, and actual form.

Working directly with paper and scissors, the designer is much like a sculptor who, although he may have a general idea or plan in mind, allows an idea to evolve progressively and naturally; in fact, there are times the material itself should be allowed to play a role in determining what the final form will be. (This should be an especial consideration of the designer who uses in his final setting newer mate-

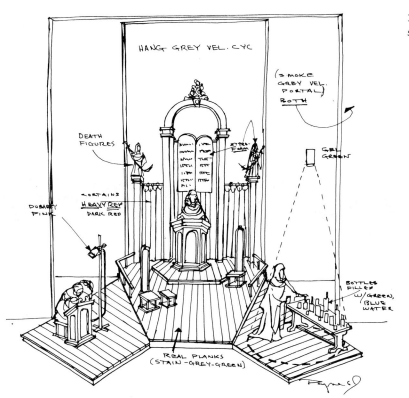

24. *Isometric drawing of
setting*

25. *Development of a scenic structure*

rials, not simulations made with the traditional wood, canvas, and paint of past stagecraft procedures.) Even though these experimental forms may at a later time be made out of heavier stronger materials, those used at this stage should be capable of easy manipulation; heavyweight paper (such as bristol board) is best suited for this work.

It must also be kept in mind that anything put on the model stage unit is automatically in a known scale. (If the model stage is ½ inch equals 1 foot, then any object placed on it becomes that scale.) A designer can, therefore, pretty much forget for the time the whole business of measurements and work for the satisfaction of his eye; that is, he can cut, assemble, and move the forms around the grid floor of the model unit until it "looks right." After this, he can measure the pieces, adjust them, if necessary, to the modular requirements of the materials used in building the actual scenery in the shop.

Of course, a designer's visual desires are always subject to the practical requirements of the scene; sight lines must be checked and the movement possibilities of the performers assured. And it should always be remembered that, even at this early experimental stage of work, the search for an exciting design should not supersede the requirements of the performers nor restrict their necessary patterns of movement merely for the sake of scenic effect. It is a wise precaution, then, even during this early period of work to keep on the model stage, along with the experimental forms being tested, a scaled figure of the human being. The designer must constantly remind himself of the relativity of any design to this human form.

Paper structures can be especially helpful when transferring actual research materials into a design. It is not often, however, that the forms the designer finds in real life will transfer directly to the stage without extensive reworking of the original construction and scale. For instance, Eugène Atget's photograph of Parisian rooftops (Fig. 26) provides good factual information which could be useful to a designer working on the first act of Puccini's La Bohème, a setting whose exterior might well resemble the view recorded by Atget. But the designer would almost certainly have to alter both the scale and architectural features of the original to suit his own needs. The complexity of planes and forms in the Atget photograph almost necessitates that the designer cut and shape this information in three-dimensional form immediately rather than sketching it out as a picture beforehand. Bristol board, as we have already noted, is the best material for this stage of work (Fig. 27). Eventually these rooftop forms must be given a more definite form and scale in addition to being integrated into the other requirements of the setting—the interior of the attic garret which the rooftop forms surround (Fig. 28).

26. Roofs in Paris, *photograph by Eugène Atget. Courtesy of The Museum of Modern Art, New York. Abbott-Levy Collection. Partial Gift of Shirley C. Burden*

Finished Paper Models

Just as rough sketches are refined so that the information they contain may be made more clear, so do rough paper structures give way to more carefully made ones. The paper model, however, can be either a step in making a more elaborate model or it can be complete in itself. The exigencies of the working theater often make it impossible for the designer to create the time-consuming exhibition model; in many instances, the paper model is more than adequate to convey the designer's intentions to those needing the information.

In making finished paper models, there are some techniques and practices that differ from those in making the heavier models which employ other materials besides paper—balsa wood, illustration board, wire, etc. Some of these differences in working procedure can be listed as follows:

1. As with the rough paper structures, bristol board (which is really a heavyweight paper stock) is the best material for paper models.

2. Paper models can be drafted all in one piece (Fig. *29a*). The thinness of the material used in these models—unlike heavier materials used in working or exhibition models—allows the bending of joints in directions not possible with illustration board; in the heavier models, thickness of material, just as with a ¾-inch thickness of an actual flat, must be

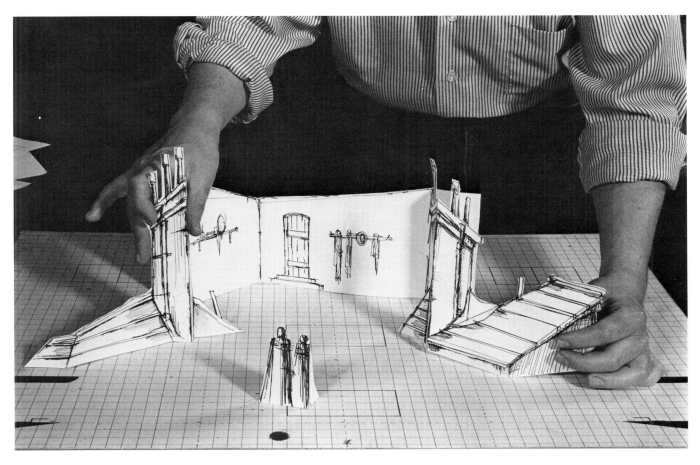

27. *Preliminary bristol board structures*

28. La Bohème *scenic model*

taken into account and compensated for. It is a common practice, also, to draft onto the more elaborate paper model details which eventually will be three-dimensional on the actual setting (or on the final model, if one is to be made). The floor plane of all paper models should be of a heavier stock than the walls and other pieces in it.

3. Paper models, unlike other types of model structures, are held to the floor plane with tabs (Fig. 29b). Rubber cement is probably the best glue for assemblage of paper models; unlike almost all other adhesives, it will not cause warpage in the paper. It is also possible to relocate glued units without damage to the paper. Excessive rubber cement is easily removed from the model when the project is completed.

4. Cutting the drafted model pattern can be done either with an X-acto knife or, with a reasonable amount of care, paper scissors.

5. The Ozalid process is the one most designers use for duplication of working drawings. It is possible to obtain a heavy paper for this process which can duplicate the designer's flat schedule directly onto a stock suitable for a paper model. This means that the same drawing which serves the shop as a working drawing for flat units can also be used to make a working paper model without the additional drafting involved when bristol board is employed. Television designers often take advantage of this

29. *Finished paper models*

timesaving step. This paper is also sturdy enough to take watercolor or designer's colors; so, with the execution of one drawing, it is possible to get a shop construction drawing, a paper model and the outline for a paint schedule.

7. Procedures and Techniques of Scenic-Model Construction

Cutting Materials

In cutting any material, two important considerations should be kept in mind: safety and accuracy. Actually, the two go hand in hand. In cutting flat materials, such as illustration board or flat balsa woods, the attitude of the designer should be similar to that of the surgeon; the right tool is necessary and rarely is the cut made all at once. Usually the first cut of the knife is made to score the material, to form a track for the later deeper cuts. Some other important practices to be observed are these:

1. Always have another piece of material under that being cut. This underpiece should be thick enough to prevent the blade going through it and scarring the surface below.

2. Always use a steel edge to guide the blade. Any other tool, such as a T square or triangle will result in damaging both the tool and quite possibly the cutter.

3. Don't try using the same blade too long; while a new blade is extremely dangerous, a dull one can be equally hazardous. The slim-barreled X-acto knife with a No. 11 blade is probably the best all-round cutting tool for boards and small pieces of wood or plastic (Fig. 8a). Its shape and size also make it an efficient tool for any carving necessary on the model.

4. For initial scoring cuts, keep the blade as close to vertical as possible. As the cutting process continues and the blade cuts deeper, more of an angle is necessary. Once again: make all cuts in progressive stages.

5. For thinner boards and papers—such as bristol board—the X-acto knife can be used but a good pair of paper shears works just as well.

6. Wire cutters are necessary for metal wires of small diameters. Wire meshes need either small tin snips, wire cutters or heavy duty scissors. Metal rods can be cut best with a small triangular rat-tail file. (See Figure 8 for illustrations of these tools.)

7. Small pieces of balsa can be cut with the X-acto knife, but for heavier balsa pieces, the razor saw, also an X-acto Company product, is recommended (Fig. 8b).

8. In preparing floor pieces which attempt to simulate tile, planks, stone pieces, etc., the best practice

is not to cut each of the component parts separately and then glue them to another board, but to cut the desired pattern into a single thickness of 100-weight illustration board in the manner demonstrated in Figure 30. The cuts shown there go only halfway through the material. In order to create a desired pattern, such as the planks being cut in the illustration, it is necessary to make two parallel cuts and then to remove the small piece between the lines. This cut should then be sanded out with the edge of a small piece of fine sandpaper folded several times to form a narrow but stiff abrasive edge (Fig. 30a).

9. The most effective tool for making small holes is the small battery-powered drill similar to the one shown in Figure 31. These tools also come with other bits which can be used in carving, routing, or sanding. They are very useful pieces of equipment and worth the initial investment.

Joining Materials and Assembly Techniques

A great deal of care and thought must be exercised in assembling the various parts of the model; bonding is extremely important. Yet there is no one bonding material suitable for all operations. Some of the more common materials and procedures are listed as follows:

Bonding Paper to Paper or Paper to Paper Boards— Rubber cement is best for this purpose. It does not

30. *Cutting illustration board into patterns*

31. *Battery-powered drill*

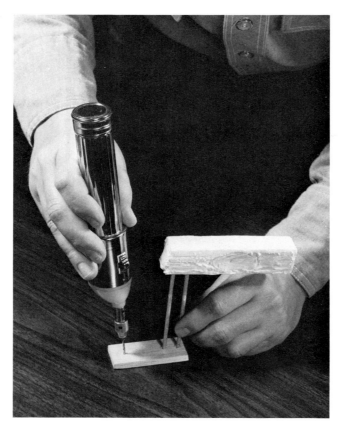

wrinkle when light papers are attached to other light papers or even to heavier stock. For the various types of rubber cement bonds, follow the instructions on the container. Glues with water bases (paste, Elmer's glue, etc.) will invariably cause warpage. Never use paste, for that matter, for anything. Acetate glues can be used in certain cases but this practice is overkill for paper and is really not satisfactory.

Bonding Paper to Balsa Woods or Metal Surfaces— Acetate glues are almost a must for this type of bonding. It is, however, possible to use aerosol spray adhesives such as Scotch Spra-ment, but these should be used with care. This type of adhesive works well when applying metal foil to wood or paperboard surfaces. Follow directions on the container to the letter.

Bonding Textures and Three-Dimensional Materials to Flat Surfaces.—In most cases, light-textured materials can be attached to surfaces with gesso or by embedding them into modeling paste; sand, string, lightweight wire meshes or strands, small twigs, etc., can all be adhered in this manner without first gluing them to the surface with other types of adhesives. Nevertheless, after they are adhered, paint over the entire surface with another coat of gesso.

Bonding Balsa Wood to Balsa Wood and to Other Materials—For the best bond between balsa woods and heavy material such as illustration board, an acetate glue (Duco cement made by Du Pont is a good product) is almost mandatory. Many of the special glues developed by model-making companies which purport to be especially manufactured for wood-to-plastic or plastic-to-plastic bonds are not entirely satisfactory; in fact, they often do not hold as well as ordinary all-purpose glues such as Duco cement. Special cements for gluing Styrofoam to Styrofoam or Styrofoam to other materials are practically worthless. But since acetate glues tend to melt most foam products, any Styrofoam piece should first be entirely coated with gesso, allowed to dry and then bonded with an acetate glue. In many cases, permanent holding pins will be necessary to give strength to a joint or bond.

For special detailed work such as window units, bars, grillwork, etc., the following pattern of work is suggested:

1. Draft the unit onto lightweight illustration board (No. 300) as shown in Figure *32a*.

2. Cut and pin the materials to the drafted pattern with dressmaker's pins (Figure *32b*).

3. Either put small amounts of glue over the joints or, preferably, glue each joint of the unit piece by piece, applying a little more glue over the juncture after all the work is completed. Allow the unit to dry and then remove any holding pins. Since some glue will invariably drip onto the illustration-board pattern under the joints, the unit will proba-

bly have to be carefully cut away from the board with a sharp X-acto knife using a No. 11 blade.

4. The unit will gain strength when coated with gesso.

5. For the transparent part of window units, use lightweight sheet acetate glued to the back. A *very* light coat of flat spray-white will allow special painting to be done on the window, such as simulating dirty glass, cracked panes, or stained glass. Rosco dyes, used for painting projection slides, is recommended for stained-glass effects.

NOTE: An inexpensive biology probe and tweezers (Figure *8i* and *j*) are handy tools for placing and holding small members of an intricate unit in place. The probe is also useful for creating priming holes in tough materials (such as 100-weight illustration board) when permanent holding pins are required.

Applying Heavy Coatings and Textures

1. Gesso is best applied with a No. 4 or 6 flat red sable brush kept for that purpose only, although some designers prefer pointed brushes rather than flat. While it will not retain its usefulness as a painting tool, an older brush which is no longer suitable for watercolor work is still serviceable for applying gesso. It must be washed out, however, immediately after use since gesso dries quickly. A gesso brush will last several years if carefully maintained.

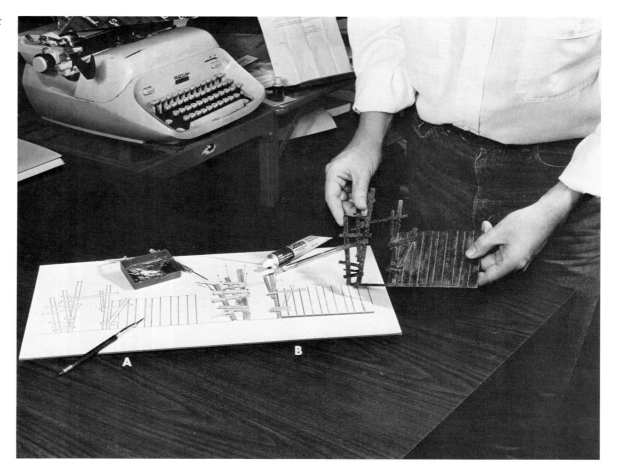

(All brushes should be cleaned in cold or tepid water; hot water ruins the bristles of any good brush.) When applying the gesso coat to a model, attempt to give a slight texture to the surface rather than striving for one that is completely smooth. This slightly textured surface tends to catch light in such a way as to give the model a greater illusion of solidity and will give a better idea of how the full-scale setting will appear. It is something of the same principle as applying broken painted textures and patterns—such as spattering—to flat surfaces; the effect causes these surfaces to appear more solid (Fig. 33).

2. If heavier textures are desired, other materials can be applied to the surface of the model at the same time as the gesso. For instance, plastic sand can be introduced into the gesso as the basic coat is being applied. This is done by (A) dipping the brush into the gesso and then (B) dipping the wet brush carefully into a small portion of the sand. This mixture can then be applied onto the desired surface with the results being as shown in Figure 34. It is possible to build up very heavy effects in this manner. Other materials—such as string, wire, cloth, or small pieces of foam or balsa—can also be applied to the model surfaces and affixed in the same manner; for light materials the gesso will act as both a binder and covering agent. For heavier materials, however, the material should be glued to

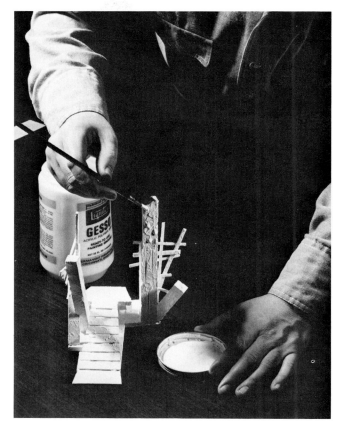

33. *Application of gesso*

34. *Sand texture on scenic model:* Home

the surface beforehand and then, when the glue is set, be covered with the gesso coating. Figure *35* shows some textures possible for scenic models.

3. For even heavier textures than possible with gesso, acrylic modeling paste is necessary (Fig. *35c*). This material allows the designer to create heavily molded forms and surfaces not attainable with gesso (Fig. *36*). If this material is applied too thickly, however, there is a tendency for it to form cracks as it dries. The best practice is to build up the form or surface in several successive layers, allowing each to dry adequately before the next layer is applied. Even with this precaution, though, some cracks will occur. These are fairly easily corrected, however, by filling them with more paste when the object is completely dried. Modeling paste, unlike gesso, must be applied with tools other than brushes; oil painting knives—which come in a variety of sizes and shapes (see Fig. *81*)—are the best tools for this purpose. It is also advisable to have a well-defined understructure before applying the paste so that it will be no thicker than necessary; Styrofoam is an easily worked material for creating these irregular forms. It is also a good practice, after the paste is applied, to coat the dried form with gesso which has a slightly tougher surface than modeling paste in addition to taking paint better.

NOTE: It is possible to duplicate almost the exact texture specified in a model (Fig. *37*) in full-scale

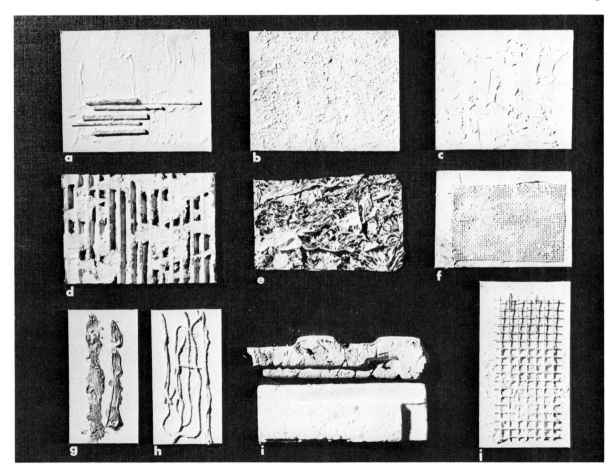

35. *Scenic-model textures: a, gesso on illustration board over balsa wood; b, gesso with plastic sand; c, modeling paste; d, gesso on corrugated board; e, gesso on metal foil; f, gesso over wire screening; g, liquid solder; h, gesso over string; i, gesso over Styrofoam; j, gesso over wire mesh*

36. *Application of modeling paste:* Cyrano de Bergerac

37. La Bohème *scenic model*

8. *Detail of setting:* La
   Bohème

scenery (Fig. *38*) with a number of new materials now in use in scenery building shops. These three-dimensional textures are accomplished in the scene shop in several ways:

1. For heavy carved forms and moldings (Fig. *38a*) sheet Styrofoam (which comes in standard sizes of 1 inch by 2 feet by 8 feet, and 2 inches by 2 feet by 8 feet, in addition to blocks of various sizes) can be easily cut and shaped with simple hand-tools and heavy sandpaper.

2. For heavy overall textures—such as plaster or stone surfaces—polyurethane foam comes in a pressurized can (which can be sprayed directly onto a surface) or can be purchased unmixed and combined in the shop so that the foam can be either cast or poured. Figure *38b* shows poured foam used to simulate piled snow. Figure *39* shows the effect of heavily applied spray foam.

All these materials are lightweight, inexpensive when compared with other materials needed to obtain the same results, and take paint easily (although it is usually much easier and quicker to spray paint these surfaces than using brushes to cover them). All foam surfaces, however, should be sealed with water-base paint before applying any acetone-based paint such as those available in aerosol cans. For additional material on using foams and plastics to achieve three-dimensional surfaces and forms, see chapter 10, *Designing and Painting for the Theatre,* by Lynn Pecktal.

39. *Use of spray foam on scenery:* Suddenly Last Summer

Force-Drying Applied Surfaces and Textures

All the materials used for model textured surfaces air-dry in a reasonable amount of time. The drying process can be, however, speeded up if necessary. Gesso, for instance, can be force-dried without unduly cracking the surface or warping the forms by putting the coated objects into a very low temperature oven with the door left open. A hand-held, blowing hair dryer is also useful in drying a gesso painted surface quickly. Care must be taken, though, that the drying process is not too rapid since this would cause warpage, especially to flat surfaces painted with gesso. This is even more true of force-drying objects or surfaces coated with modeling paste.

Finishing the Exhibition Model

The painting of an exhibition model is not very different in approach from the manner in which a scenic sketch is made. Much of the technique, if not all the materials, is similar; in both instances, however, a number of like principles operate. Perhaps it would not be time wasted to review some of those techniques and principles before going on to the finishing of the exhibition model. The three most important principles in making a set sketch could be summarized as follows:

1. Build up the work in layers, from background forward.

2. The progression of the sketch should be from mass to detail. (That is, lay in the large elements of an object before superimposing the painted detail over it.)

3. Highlight the details last; deeper shadows can also be added at this time.

In other words, do not paint the sketch "by the numbers" in the manner of the painting kits available from hobby shops where the canvas is broken into a myriad of small individual shapes each with a number, the painter's task being merely to match each shape with a correspondingly numbered tube of paint. Most painters, in fact, count on the underlying layers of paint to give quality and depth of surface to each of the subsequent ones. Special effects both in the designer's studio work and in the final scene painting on the actual scenery often depend on the transparency of these various layers of paint. In its simplest form, the scenic sketch can be outlined as follows (Fig. *40*):

1. Define outline on white material. (Illustration board or heavy watercolor paper is preferable to lighterweight materials.) The surface of any watercolor material is very important; it should not be too slick—such as the almost glossy surface found on hot-press illustration board—or too highly textured. Most designers over a period of time develop an af-

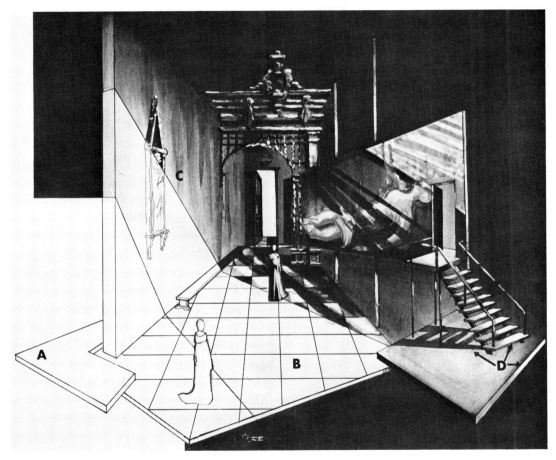

finity to one type of paper or board over another; experimentation with various materials will reveal this preference.

2. The basic tonality (either watercolor or pastel can be used) is laid over the entire outline. In any technique used, certain large effects can be created at this stage. In the drawings of Robert Edmond Jones, the direction of the Conte crayon is clearly visible in the final sketch; in this preliminary stage, he allowed this basic coat to provide much of the texture and form of the finished work. In any case, it is always desirable to let some of this background show through the overlaying coats of paint, not attempt to cover it up entirely. It is also possible to define planes and objects simply with line and minimum shading; again, practically all Robert Edmond Jones's work demonstrates the value of this technique.

3. Large masses (plus their shadows are laid over the background, usually in dark colors and with a minimum of detail differentiation).

4. Details are placed at appropriate points on the dark masses. (In most cases these details are also the highest areas and would be where the light catches on the form.)

5. Shading can then be reinforced and final highlighting added at the end.

6. It is advisable to give the entire finished rendering a light spray with a nonglossy plastic spray to seal and protect the surface.

Figure *41* shows the front view of a model based on the same design we have just been examining in the scenic sketch. Again, as we have already pointed out, the finishing of this exhibition model follows approximately the same steps as when making the scenic sketch.

All the principles apparent in Figure *40* can be directly applied to the finishing of the scenic model; most important, neither should be done piecemeal, but in successive layers. Figure *42* shows more clearly the following elements of the finished scenic model:

1. Unfinished model materials (illustration board, balsa wood, etc.).

2. Texture coat consisting of modeling paste which has also been given a coat of gesso. (For lighter textures, gesso alone might be applied to the unfinished model materials; even with gesso, a slight texture is possible.)

3. Basic tonality applied with aerosol spray paint. (In this instance, a light-colored wood stain is the paint used. This, as with most wood stains, is relatively transparent but tends to produce darker areas in the depressions of the texture coat. These differences in paint surface are often desired since it more nearly approximates paint techniques used on actual full-scale scenery.)

4. Other coats of darker aerosol sprays are very lightly added to this basic color to produce a deeper and more varied tonality. The objective, as with the

scenic sketch, is not to cover completely the surface with each successive coat, but to build up a richer surface with more depth and luminosity than is possible with a single coat of opaque spray. Most of the aerosol paints and stains have a slightly glossy finish which tends to give a more lively surface to the complete model.

5. The model can now be more deeply shaded and articulated with brush work and inks. Sepia ink is a good shading color if the effect of age is desired. Age tends to turn surfaces of materials brown; if the shading is done with washes of India ink, the effect is often that of dirt, not the passage of time. In some instances, of course, dirt is the effect desired, but in most instances, the browner, more transparent tonality provided by sepia is preferable to that of India ink. In Figure 43, the following possibilities are apparent:

6. Found images may be incorporated (which could also be incorporated into a scenic sketch) into the model. Quite often this image gives the designer his key to the basic tonality he desires; but it is also possible for the designer to tone the image with inks or watercolor. Images should be securely glued to heavier board with rubber cement when made part of a model.

7. Metallic members of the model can be left with their own color and surface unfinished; however, metal often needs a protective coating of plastic to keep it from tarnishing.

8. Final highlighting and enrichment of highly textured surfaces can be accomplished with water-soluble metallic colors now available to designers. Metallic pastes can also be used for the same purpose.

Backgrounds for the Scenic Model

The background for the model can serve two functions at once; it will, of course, be part of the model itself, but, if not permanently attached to the model floor plan, can also be used as a painter's paint schedule. It is even possible to photograph this background for use as a slide projection or it can be duplicated onto a scenic unit in the manner discussed in part 3, section 11 (see Use of Photographic Images in Full-Scale Scenic Painting). If used as the basis for painting a backdrop, an acetate sheet which has been inked into a half-inch grid will be necessary for the painter in order to reproduce the drop in full scale. The acetate grid described above in section 5 can be used for this purpose. The background can be made in several ways; two possibilities are as follows:

1. Flat pastel and watercolor renderings (Fig. 44). Pastel is the best material for obtaining atmospheric effects. (These effects can be duplicated on the stage either by a lens projector or by a Linnebach projector which requires no lens; the Linnebach is actually superior in some ways for soft-edged images, al-

43. *Other aspects of exhibition-model finishing*

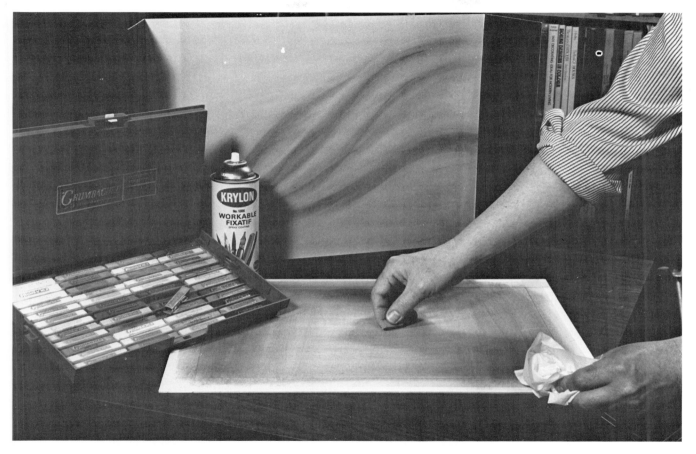

though brightness is often a serious drawback in its use.)

2. Found images can be assembled onto an illustration board backing (Fig. *45a*). If a more uniform tonality is desired, the images can be "brought together" with inks, watercolors, etc. (Fig. *45b*). The results, as with the background described above, can be reproduced in full scale by similar techniques used with any other flat design.

Set Decoration for the Scenic Model

This area of model making is often the most troublesome for the designer; the various items which comprise it are usually small in scale yet require great care in execution in order to give the desired finish to the model. On the actual stage, a designer would rarely be called upon to put crude kitchen chairs into a palace throne room; yet this is often the effect one sees in a model. The larger forms and surfaces project one feeling, the set decoration gives another. And while it is possible to obtain miniature furniture and set properties, sometimes in an actual period, they are rarely compatible with the scale used in the model and often extremely expensive. These items, therefore, must almost always be fabricated by the designer if a totality of effect is to be obtained. Let us examine some of the problems in set decoration of the model in more detail.

Furniture and Other Set Dressings

Most furniture for model settings must be made. It is possible, however, to obtain some miniature furniture in half-inch scale from the toy departments of most chain stores (although most is either too large or small). But even when the proper scale is found, most of these items must be modified to correspond to the style required (Fig. *46a*). Pictures, murals, etc., can usually be found in magazines in appropriate size, style, and color. Other items of decoration (statuary, chandeliers, etc.) must almost always be fabricated, although there are many decorative items—such as those sold for Christmas decorations—which can be modified for use in the model setting (Fig. *46b*).

Hangings and Draperies—Real fabric, no matter how sheer, will not give the same effect in the model setting as when used in the full-scale setting. It is advisable, therefore, to simulate any fabric scenic piece, such as a drape or curtain, rather than using an actual piece of fabric. It is really no problem to duplicate color; folds and textures can be indicated either by graphic techniques or built up three-dimensionally with gesso or modeling paste. The results will be much more in keeping with the scale of the model since more precise contours can be assured (Fig. *47*).

45. *Background assembled from found images*

46. *Set decoration*

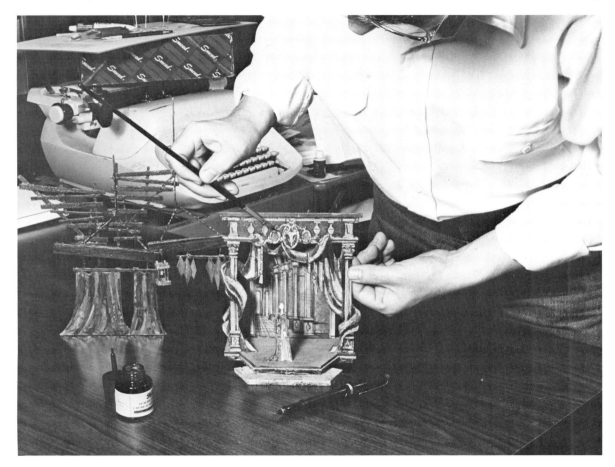

47. *Draped units for scenic models*

Foliage, Trees, and Natural Forms—Trees can be easily simulated by selection of small branches from actual trees or bushes. Foliage, bushes, etc., can also be simulated from materials obtained at model supply stores or from common household materials such as cellulose sponge. Small-scale plants must almost always be constructed. Precise cutting of various flat materials is necessary to obtain a desired effect or style of plant, although at best, the result can never be better than approximate. Figure *46c* shows a metal paper fastener being cut with heavy duty shears; the simple act of cutting the thin metal material produces the curvature of the leaves although the entire frond must be shaped when assembled with other members.

Wall and Floor Surfaces—Although it is possible to find existing textures and surfaces which could be incorporated into a model setting, more often than not, precise styles of wallpaper, carpeting, or floor finish must be simulated if proper scales are to be maintained.

Part 3 *Experimental Techniques in Scenic Models*

8. The Concept of Experimenting

Simultaneous, immediate, composite, transparent, multiple, condensed, fragmented, tangible, reconstructed— these are some of the key words. There are two others that are even more crucial: speed and space. Unexpectedly the world shrinks as it expands; there is a great deal more to see, and yet we see it faster. In trying to condense modern multiplicity into tangible form, artists have turned to certain shortcuts, to transparent, fragmented, reconstructed images where two compelling illusions—speed and space—act as basic source material. (Katharine Kuh, *Break-Up*)

Many artists of the twentieth century—painters, sculptors, printmakers, and even scene designers— have all but rejected the age-old practice of first getting a complete concept in mind and only then, using a limited number of basic materials and a restricted technique, working out that concept into a predetermined result. It is now acceptable—in fact, almost mandatory—in every art form to include techniques, materials and approaches which would have been unthinkable even a hundred years ago; the conscious use of accidental results, the breakdown of barriers between two-dimensional and three-dimensional work, and the combination of diverse elements and mediums into a single work, is now well entrenched in the common consciousness of every working artist. The reasons for these developments are many; we live in a world that mainly depends upon the assembly line for most of its needs; we have instruments which allow us to view anything in the world in a quick succession of single images or in any number of superimpositions, permutations, and scales; change and chance have become important elements in both our lives and our art. All these directions have made it increasingly apparent that the art of the twentieth century is mainly one of assemblage. The bringing together of preexisting forms and images into new contexts and configurations has been and continues to be a dominant trend; painting, music, sculpture, dance, all art forms, in fact, have been greatly influenced by the artist's seeking of new meanings out of the innovative combination of both exotic and commonplace elements.

The artist, then, is no longer forced into a prescribed pattern as to the selection of his subject matter or the manner by which he expresses that subject matter. And if there has been one overall change in the attitude toward the making of art it is that the artist thinks of himself less as a creator of works springing from the deep recesses of a singular and mysterious ego, and more as an expert assembler of images and forms gleaned from an objective world.

This more intense inspection of that objective world does not rule out the individual artist's point 61 of view; it does, however, make the old romantic vision of the artist as a remote and incomprehensible figure less viable. Few artists today insist on the premise that the most important reason behind their work is to expose their own intensely subjective, mystical state of being. Self-expression has given way to the desire to express the world outside the single individual. This world has, the artist of today realizes, an infinitely rich store of materials and experiences to offer; his purpose is not so much to call attention to his own peculiar state of mind as it is to show to others some of that richness and diversity he in his own experience has found. This is especially true for the scene designer whose work is primarily dedicated to the service of others. As a result of this desire for an expanded vision, the creation of the static, literal picture has all but given way to the ordering of forms, objects, colors, textures, light, and time—all derived from the objective world—into a fourth-dimensional flux. The designer's job is no longer the making of imitative illustrations; it is nothing less than the assembly and management of images in time.

In the following sections we will be dealing with the aspects of the designer's art which cannot be completely outlined nor shown in step-by-step illustrations. All that can be done is to raise a few basic questions concerning the type and nature of experimental work possible with scenic models in the studio and to suggest some of the tools and materials which could be used in this work. The whole basis of this activity rests, however, in the word "creative play." This concept merely holds that the designer should, in his continuing practice, allow for periods of time in which his work is not directly project-oriented (that is, being done for a specific production during a specific segment of time), but is geared only toward exploring the random possibilities which present themselves to him through accidental and undirected experimentation. Creative play is, next to actually experimenting on a full-scale stage, the most positive and active way of increasing a designer's sensitivity and awareness to the vast potential which exists in the world outside the stage door; a world which he must never stop exploring. Moreover, this is an activity not meant for student days alone; it is one which no designer ever outgrows. If the designer does not make an active and continuing effort to expand his vision through experimentation, he will soon be caught up in an ever-decreasing circle of past solutions, the result of which can only be an increasingly sterile imitation of his own vital work.

For the purposes of explanation, this part will be divided into three areas of investigation: the use of found images in the scenic model; the use of found objects and materials as the basis for a scenic model; the various ways 35-mm projections and projection equipment can be used in the designer's creative work. These categories, however, used either separately or in combination, offer literally an infinite scope to the practice of scene design. (For additional information and discussion of the underlying principles and philosophies presented herein, please see the Bibliography.)

9. Use of Existing Images

The found image often serves as the basis for three-dimensional scenic units. The source of Jocelyn Herbert's figure of Christ (Fig. *48*) used in the John Osborne play, *Luther,* is obviously derived from Grünewald's painting of the Crucifixion (Fig. *49*).

This image, however, can be used in ways other than as research source material or as a single pictorial unit. It can, as shown in Figures *50* through *52,* be incorporated into a design in ways which integrate its flat rectangular form into a more dynamic arrangement:

Several things are immediately evident in this simple exercise. Perhaps the most important point to be observed, though, is that while a precise meaning cannot be ascribed to each of these variations, it is obvious that the basic perception of the

48. *Detail of setting for* Luther

49. The Crucifixion *by*
Grünewald

image is greatly altered in each case. And while few would agree as to exact emotion or message these variations project, it is safe to say that each sends a specifically different signal to the spectator. It is a very short step from the observation of this abstract principle to a concrete application of it. This is not to say, as some basic texts in design tend to imply, that curved lines always mean comedy, tall vertical ones denote tragedy, and so on. Nevertheless, it is basically a sound principle that particular forms can help project more forcefully concepts that are essentially literary rather than visual. But these forms must be tailored to support very specific problems; their size and shape do not inherently carry exact meanings.

Let us take, as an example, the first scene of Shakespeare's *Richard III*. At the beginning of the play, Richard states very definitely his ambitions—to get the throne of England from his brother, Edward IV (or from anyone who happens to stand in succession to it) by any means possible. At the moment, however, Edward is still king and at the height of his power. This relationship can be made visually evident by showing Richard standing below a large image of Edward. (The approach we are taking in this example is not a realistic one, but rather a theatrical one.) By juxtaposing this image, along with Richard and perhaps the actual throne on which Edward sits, we have both the objective and the ob-

50. *Grünewald image used in scenic model*

51. *Variation of same Grünewald image*

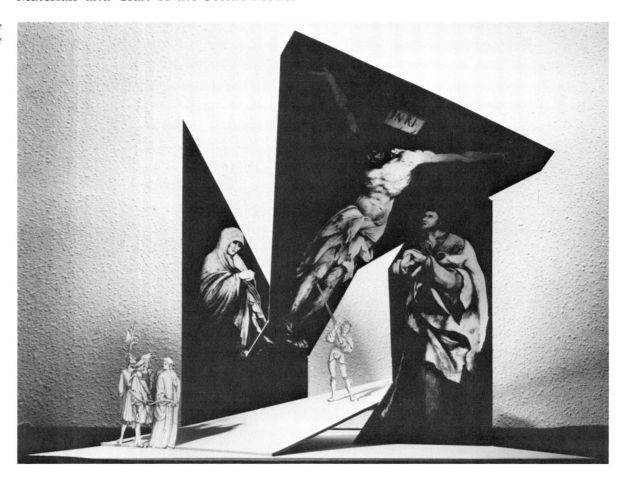

stacle to Richard's ambition in plain view. We could present these elements on the stage in the manner shown in Figure 53.

But does this really show all we want to say; is the nature of the scene in any way furthered by this arrangement? The design is a formally balanced one; in a word, it is static. But the play is, if nothing else, a long series of brutal confrontations, plots, and betrayals; in another word, it is dynamic. Even this first scene is fraught with the violent intensity that marks the rest of the play. We need, therefore, a scenic environment which will reflect and support both the active nature of the play and savage undercurrent of this scene in particular. What is required is something which visually presents Edward's initial eminence while at the same time introducing us to the dangerous directions Richard intends to pursue in his path to the throne. Using the same elements—the overscaled image and the throne, we can create another configuration which might better support the action of this particular scene (Fig. 54).

Here, several important changes have been made from our first design; the image has been, to begin with, cut in half with a long diagonal line and separated to allow passage between the two parts. (We do, in fact, tend to read qualities of action into lines which have no other representational function; a vertical line does have a feeling of stability and order; a horizontal line is perceived to be in a state

52. *Variation of same Grünewald image*

53. *Design for* Richard III

of rest; a diagonal line, such as the one imposed on the image of Edward, is the most active of the three and can be read as unstable and falling. Actually, since Richard has, at the beginning of the play, already given much thought to his ambitions, he has, in effect, already begun the process of toppling the king; that is, pushing him from the vertical toward the horizontal. In fact, the last time we see Edward he is headed for his deathbed as a direct result of Richard's plottings.) It is through this broad slash, then, that the figure of Richard first emerges. Even he, according to Shakespeare's own internal evidence, is incapable of standing up straight due to his congenital deformities. And, when we first see him, the dangerously pointed form above him helps to emphasize the dangerous course he has decided for himself; of course which could, if he does not play his hand correctly, cost him not only the throne but his head. In addition, the throne is now some distance from his entrance and the way to it at an oblique angle to him, not directly in his path. Even though an audience will not immediately say to itself, "Ah, yes, I see: this design is saying to me that . . . ," it will receive information that visually underscores the scene better than the first static picture; the split image of Edward becomes more vulnerable as it becomes more active and the throne becomes an actual objective in space as well as in time.

The use of found images, either painted or projected, either in actual scale or overscaled, is likely to remain part of the designer's iconography for some time to come. And there are good reasons why this should be so. There are, however, some cautionary principles which should be observed in their use. Few actors, for instance, would ever consider going in front of an audience and shouting, "Hey, you out there—look at me!" And yet this is the exact effect produced in many designs using images when they were not carefully integrated into the production as a whole. In the past twenty years, many designers have believed themselves automatically to be modern and up-to-date by the simple inclusion of projected images into their work. The results, however, are often totally disastrous for all involved. No performer can hope to retain the attention of an audience if he and an image fifty times his size must fight for the focus. Especially in the use of greatly overscaled images, their purpose must be thoroughly considered and their effect carefully managed. A good example of how effective such images can be when integrated into the total design exists in Sergei Eisenstein's *Ivan the Terrible, Part I* (Fig. 55).

It was part of Eisenstein's scenic concept to have the characters of the drama constantly under the scrutiny of the great searching eyes of Russian iconic faces. But, it is important to note, these images always take their place in the total design; they never "upstage" the performers. They do, in fact, help us focus not so much on where a scene is taking place but what is happening in that locale. The fact that this example is taken from the cinema does not alter the principle exposed here. A less successful use of the overscaled human face was employed in a Russian production of *My Poor Marat*, by Alexei Arbuzov (Fig. *56*). Here, the performers all but fade into the scenic background.

While these admonitions may seem to indicate an unduly cautious attitude toward the experimental use of images, the fact remains that most designers and directors do attempt to make sure that anything they introduce into the production "pays its way," that no single element is allowed to distort the balance of the whole. Images can do much to further the meaning of a production, but while they may very much aid and amplify the work of a performer, and the playwright, they should never supplant it.

10. Found Objects and Materials

To a very large extent, no designer can avoid using in his work objects that already exist. In interior settings especially, whether period or modern, he is expected to assemble appropriate items as part

55. *Still photograph from* Ivan the Terrible

56. *Setting for Arbuzov's My Poor Marat*

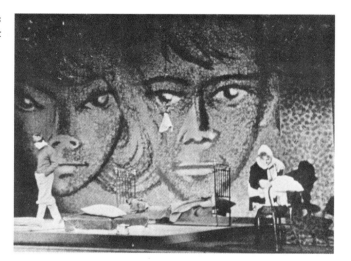

of the design—furniture, set properties, and set dressing. Since many of his designs deal with particular characters in a specific environment, part of his skill depends on the development of a sensitivity to the precise atmospheres that a collection of preexisting objects can evoke. Even when designing settings where furniture and set dressing have little part, he is expected to understand the visual language that results from the juxtaposition of objects and performers. For the fact of the matter is, that objects—singularly and in groups—can and do speak. The language, of course, is different from that of words, but it is no less eloquent or exact than that of the actor. It is, in fact, often part of the designer's function to send to an audience complex and meaningful signals by the use of an object or a configuration of objects. And while these messages are not necessarily perceived by that audience on conscious levels (indeed, what is conveyed in this manner should not be an obvious statement), they can amplify an actor's role or clarify a director's viewpoint in situations where words would be inadequate. More importantly, they can, and very often do, enrich the play's meaning and the author's intent. Any designer who has worked in the theater even for a short period of time begins to see the potential of objective form in making even complicated ideas clear and meaningful. One example will suffice here:

In 1967, the National Theater of Great Britain produced Chekhov's *Three Sisters.* It was directed by Lawrence Olivier and designed by Josef Svoboda. (Pictures of this production can be seen in Richard Pilbrow's book, *Stage Lighting*, and the entire production was filmed and distributed for the 1973–74 American Theatre Film Festival.) While the basic settings were not realistic, the furniture and set properties were in period; these, however, although few, were carefully considered, both as to their placement and their dramatic purpose. One set property used in the setting for acts 1 and 2 (the same locale), was given a special function to perform. This piece was an ornate clock made in the likeness of a city cathedral; a building one might expect to find in some great Russian city. Ostensibly the clock was simply a highly decorative but essentially utilitarian item; no one ever actually wound it, called attention to it directly, or even acknowledged its presence in the room. To the casual observer, this clock would appear to be nothing more nor less than what it was: something that most drawing rooms of the period might have had and something any designer decorating this setting might use. Yet, as the play progressed, this clock began to play an active part in the unfolding of the drama. It helped in a very positive way to underscore one of the underlying themes in this play; that life passes most people by, that if there is any excitement or gaiety

to be had out of it, it is always in some other place. For the characters of *Three Sisters,* this better existence can only be had in a large city; in this case, Moscow. By combining the element of time (and consequently making it a constant reminder of its passage) with an image which also reminded this group of the glittering life they were missing, Svoboda created a potent symbol which made its point without intruding on the action of the play. Even the placement of the clock on the stage, set alone as it was on its own high pedestal helped to reveal the fears and obsessions of the characters who inhabit the room with it. In the film version, this image became stronger than in the stage version; at one time, the camera slowly panned across the room and came to rest on the clock. When the camera stopped, the image was out of focus; but as the chimes struck the hour, the picture cleared and gave the spectator a closeup view of this time-passing city-life symbol. There was no mistake as to the message being sent to the audience; the point was subtly but forcefully made. Objects, as we have said before, can speak; and what they say is often more eloquent and powerful than any words could ever be.

It is with this attitude in mind that the designer learning his craft should approach his experiments with found objects; he must look for the various ways in which he can combine abstract concepts with concrete forms, colors, and textures. He is not simply charged with the decoration of the stage space, he should think of his profession as one where the poetic and dramatic values of a production are transmitted in large part by his manipulation of elements taken from the objective world. The designer should also be in constant touch with the work being done in other arts. Much of the work being done there can have a significant influence on his own. Constructions, such as Edward Keinholz's assemblage and mixed media work at the Whitney Museum of American Art show how powerful statements can be composed of essentially simple elements (Fig. 57). This type of construction is not unlike those which the designer is required to make; the student of design can learn much by keeping abreast of the work of such artists as Keinholz who use the commonplace and familiar to create evocative and meaningful configurations.

Model makers in particular should be familiar with the work of one of America's most important artists of the past four decades, Joseph Cornell. He was an extremely sensitive artist who created a sizeable body of work from a wide variety of simple forms and materials. His work is closely related to the type of experimentation that is being suggested here (Fig. 58).

The natural tendency for most designers is to collect; images, objects, materials—everything, in fact, that has tactile or visual interest has a peculiar fascination for those who make their living exploring the possibilities and potentials of the physical world. This is a necessary quality that all designers should have to a great degree, and one that must be fostered continually. It is wise, therefore, in the designer's student days to begin to make provision for ways to keep this ever-growing multifaceted collection vital and constantly available. A good principle to foster in this: never come back to your studio without bringing something with you; perhaps an interesting twig or a piece of rusted metal. Nobody outside the profession will ever quite understand (except those in other visual arts); but then, that is one of the reasons they are not designers.

It is impossible to suggest further just what the designer should collect or how he might go about using those things he does; notwithstanding the wide range of possible materials that present themselves to his attention every day, certain preferences will always come to the fore, both as to the nature of the material and its arrangement on the model stage. Some designers are partial to organic form and will always emphasize it in their work, while others will lean toward the architectonic; what they find and how they use it will probably continue to reflect these predispositions. But there is no better way to break old engrained habits and prejudices than by removing the necessity of having to put to formal use the results of these experiments. If the

57. *Assemblage by Edward Keinholz:* The Wait. *Courtesy of the Collection of the Whitney Museum of American Art, New York. Geoffrey Clements Photography, Staten Island*

58. *Assemblage by Joseph Cornell:* Sun Box. *Courtesy of Alvin S. Lane*

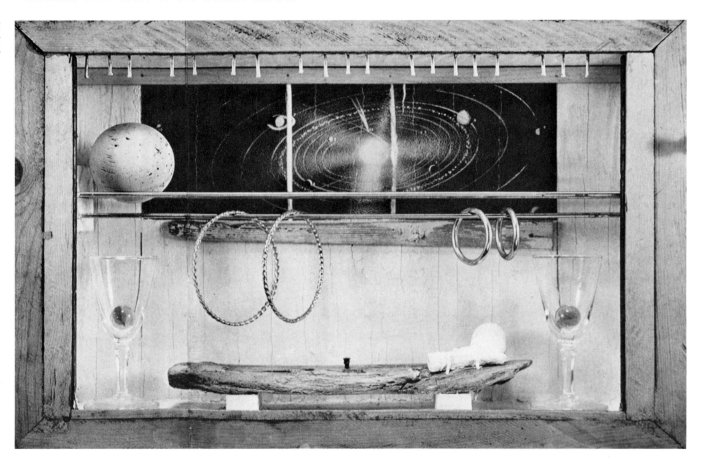

designer is not under the pressure of having to devise a design for an actual proposed production, he is apt to be more open to change and adventurous in testing new visual ideas. All working designers know how tempting it is to stick with those design solutions which have proved effective in the past, and how increasingly difficult it is to predict the success of a new idea. Undirected as this type of work might seem to be, it can have positive effects on a designer's future creations. For example a piece of scrap electrical equipment can, when put into a relationship with the human figure, suggest two completely different scenic possibilities to the designer's imagination as shown in Figures 59 and 60. In short, an integral part of the designer's craft must be a driving sensitivity to the entire world in which he lives; moreover, he must keep this sensitivity in constant operation: the working designer works all the time.

Much of the raw material of the scenic designer's art is, of course, to be found in the various museums our civilization maintains; but that is not his exclusive source. And although most designers love those repositories which house the world's greatest cultural achievements, there must exist an equal passion for the more negative aspects of human accomplishment: the junkyard, the tenement, in fact, all the broken and discarded elements of our various cultures. Much of what we focus on in the theater takes place not with or within the finest examples of our art but in the derelict remains of our society. There should be, simply, no visual, tactile, or auditory phenomena outside the all-pervading attention of the designer. And while the selection of a play almost always precedes a design for it, the designer, in his day-to-day exposure to the world as a whole, should never miss the opportunity to let his imagination have free play, to "assign" a play or opera to a compelling visual image which might accidently capture that all-pervading attention. For instance, Figure 61 shows the interior of a small freestanding fireplace which has been affected by years of use; its particular qualities might, to the discerning eye, provide an evocative scenic concept for a Greek play—perhaps *Electra*. It even suggests an alternative plan to the usual placement of the permanent architectural features of such a play: the door to the palace might be put to one side (A) rather than in the center, its customary position.

The scenic designer would do well to keep in mind Herman Melville's astute observation that "poetry is not a thing of ink and rhyme, but of thought and act, and, in the later way, is by any one to be found anywhere, when in useful action sought."

59. *Experimental scenic model*

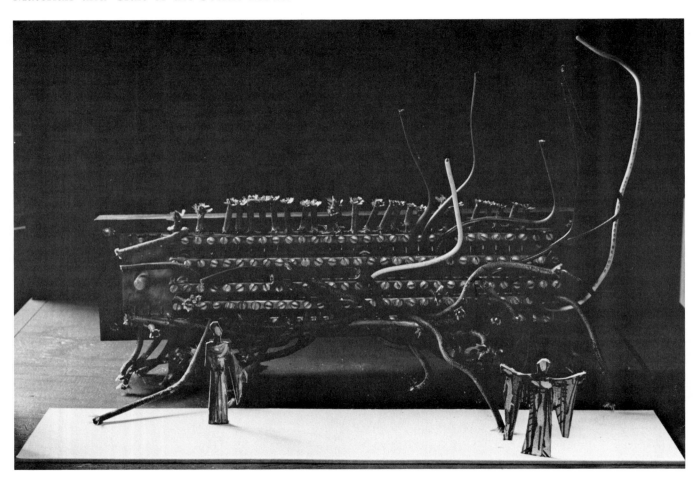

60. *Experimental scenic model (variation)*

61. *Experimental scenic model (variation)*

11. Use of 35-mm Projection for Experimental Work

There are a number of ways the designer can use 35-mm slide projections. Not only do they allow him to record his productions for a permanent collection of past projects, they can also assist him in the creative process of designing a production. Perhaps it would be advantageous at this point to list the most important ways the 35-mm projection and projection equipment can be employed by the designer in his work before dealing with some of those categories in more depth.

1. To record the finished production most designers either have their work photographed or do it themselves. A 35-mm camera and projector are very wise investments for any designer, especially if he seeks research materials directly, as when traveling to a foreign country. It is also a wise precaution to have all models and finished set sketches photographed in both black and white as well as in color. Most designers do not wish to incur the expense of sending large bulky portfolios to prospective employers; a careful selection of prints of models, set sketches, and production photos brought together in a careful presentation sells the designer much better than a bulging package of past work.

2. In the studio, highly evocative possibilities result from the projection of slides (of every sort and subject) on basic forms and textures. This process can be one of the most experimental and productive stages of the design exploration. It can also provide a positive form of creative play for the designer even when he has no specific project in mind; the results of this work might very well solve specific problems at a later time. (A more complete discussion of this process follows this outline.)

3. Images either selected or created can be photographed onto slides and used either as projections in the actual production or as an aid in duplicating them in a larger scale. (A more complete discussion of this process follows this outline.)

4. While we are not dealing with final renderings in this text, one method of making such a drawing (in lieu of traditional perspective drawing techniques) is to finish the model, photograph it onto a 35-mm slide, and then project it onto a piece of blank white illustration board. This process makes it possible to trace the outline in pencil with great accuracy. Figure 63 is a drawing made in this manner from the model shown in Figure 62.

Projection on Basic Forms and Surfaces

While it is not possible to outline completely all the ways in which this experimentation might be conducted, a few basic directions can be suggested here. What causes differing effects will always be

62. *Photographic slide of scenic model*

63. *Scenic sketch made from photographic slide*

dependent, of course, upon the surface onto which the images are projected. These surfaces will in large part determine the quality and "message" of the image as perceived by an audience; scrims and other fabrics, granular surfaces, fractured forms, linear groupings, all give markedly different effects. In Figure 64 we have a basic arrangement of forms. Figures 65 through 68 demonstrate how changed this same arrangement becomes when different images are projected onto it.

But while many of the resulting designs created by this method could be duplicated on the actual stage with larger projectors than those used in the studio, we are not limited to projections alone to secure the final result; these experiments might very well serve as the basis for determining designs which would be painted on scenic units, not projected. Figure 69 shows a model composed of forms onto which an image has been projected; Figure 70 is a similar model but the image, in this instance, has been painted directly on the forms. This method, then, provides the designer with interesting distortions which he could never "think" out on his own. One of the most positive reasons, in fact, why he should experiment with projects on his small model stage is that even the most inventive designer could never predict all the results obtainable by simple alteration in the distance, direction, and surface form to which an image may be subjected.

Use of Photographic Images in Full-Scale Scenic Painting

There is a relatively simple yet effective way by which a small pre-existing image can be accurately duplicated on a larger scale. It is essentially the same process discussed above which demonstrated how an image of the scenic model could be used as a basis for making a scenic sketch (Figs. 62 and 63). The steps in the procedure recommended here are uncomplicated and can be mastered quickly. The following outline of these steps should explain the technique sufficiently.

1. Select desired image. Line drawings, such as the one used in the model shown in Figure 71, give the best results, although the technique is not limited to this type of image alone. If the image is exceptionally atmospheric, that is, if the lines of the objects and forms in it are indistinct, accurate duplication will of course be more difficult. Nevertheless, the basic scale and outline of the image can probably be better ascertained and more quickly laid out than when using the more customary grid of the painter's elevation.

2. A 35-mm slide must be made of the selected image. This slide must be extremely sharp and clear if the best results are to be obtained in the scene shop.

3. The slide can then be projected onto any prepared surface (Fig. 72).

*64. Basic scenic-model
forms*

65. *Projection on basic forms*

*66. Projection on
basic forms*

68. *Projection on basic forms*

69. *Experimental scenic model*

70. *Design derived from experimental model:* Aïda, *tomb scene*

The size of the image, naturally, will depend on how far the projector is from the surface of the scenic unit; a 3-inch lens, however, gives a bigger image closer to the projection surface than will a 5-inch lens. Since the size of the projected image is dependent upon the distance from the projection surface, for large single works, such as a backdrop, it is advisable to divide the basic picture into segments, photographing each segment individually. Alignment of the separate parts back into the total image is not a difficult task if small key marks are made on the original picture.

4. It is a simple matter, even for those not trained in scene-painting technique, to follow the lines of the image with great accuracy. For larger images, where several painters might be required, it is wise to have them periodically trade off areas on which they are working. This is a practice that even professional scene painters use; it prevents the idiosyncrasies of painting style, which no painter can avoid, from showing up too boldly in isolated areas. The general lighting of the area where the painting is to take place must, of course, be darker than when regular scene painting is being done. Figure 73 shows the finished unit in the actual setting.

5. This technique can also be used to project and duplicate distortions of the original image. This can be done by simply moving the projector to whatever angle gives the desired effect. Superimposition and

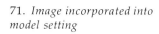

71. *Image incorporated into model setting*

72. *Technique for scenic
painting of image*

multiple images may also be obtained by use of the projector. This can be done either by projecting the image onto the surface, painting it, and then projecting the second over the painted image. Using two projectors at once is possible, but it is often much more difficult to paint effectively the resulting image; the increased amount of light from the two projectors tends to fade both images to the point where accurate rendering of the painted image becomes a problem.

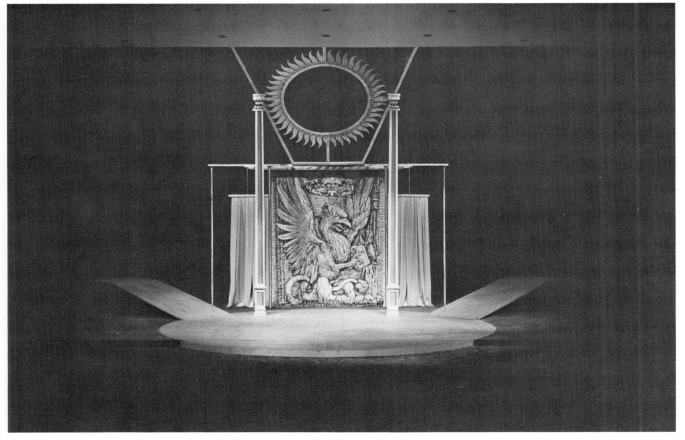

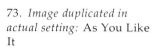

73. *Image duplicated in actual setting:* As You Like It

Part 4 *Photographing Scenic Models*

12. Notes and Suggestions by
Elliott Mendelson

The main problem in photographing model sets is creating the illusion of depth while maintaining a strong feeling for the dramatic impact desired by the scenic designer. In this brief chapter, a few of the basic principles which have been developed over the past few years will be illustrated. It should be understood from the beginning that these are very basic principles and each photographic assignment may require slight modifications to achieve the best possible image.

The first step in making a model photograph is to discuss with the designer the various aspects of the set which are deemed important. From this discussion, a clearer understanding of motivation, direction and personal feeling about the design can be discerned. Most designers will indicate a desire to re-create the impression one gets from seeing the actual set being used on a stage during a performance. While this can be achieved with much difficulty and expense, due to technical problems, a more direct approach to a single objective will prove just as beneficial. To this end decide whether the photograph is to be a record of the physical layout of the set's elements or a dramatic interpretation of the effects created by lighting.

What we see in black-and-white photographs is the sum total of all the images created by the bright and dark areas of the image. If in the model all the dark areas are eliminated (no shadows), the remaining image would be void of all form (Fig. 74). If, on the other hand, the dark areas are increased to the point where one shadow intersects the other, the original forms would not be rendered accurately (Fig. 75).

The first step in lighting a model is to provide separation between each of the set's elements by providing good lighting balance between the bright and the dark areas (contrast ratio [Fig. 76]).

In Figure 77 note that one light (fill) is located at the camera position. It is important that the quality of this light remain soft and produce no shadows on the set. The function of this lamp is to provide adequate illumination to record the image of the set on film. The softness of this lamp can be controlled by placing a translucent material in front of the light. By moving this defuser closer to the model, the quality of the light becomes softer. Once in place a light meter reading can be made using the incident method to determine the proper exposure. Exposure and subsequent film development will be discussed later.

The next light to be placed is the key light. Unlike the fill light, the quality of light from this lamp should be harsh and produce marked shadows on the sets. It is this light source which will produce

74. *Flat-lighting effect:*
Cyrano de Bergerac

74. *Flat-lighting effect:*
Cyrano de Bergerac

76. *Lighting for form*

the separation between each of the major set elements. The position of this lamp is critical. Good separation can usually be obtained by placing this light source to the rear and to one side of the model. Elevate the lamp until the desired shadow length is achieved. Normally, the elevation of the lamp is such that it throws a beam of light at a 45-degree angle to the horizontal plane of the set. The intensity of this lamp should not be more than one stop greater than the fill light when both are measured using the incident method.

After some experimentation, satisfactory results should be obtainable in making a record photograph of the model using the two-light method described above. More dramatic effects are obtainable when: the contrast ratio between the key and fill light is increased; the angle of the key light is altered; or additional lighting equipment supplements the existing setup. One should be careful at this point not to add too many additional lights, as the shadows they produce will only tend to confuse rather than add dramatic impact or clarify the final picture. One method used to enhance a particular area of the design is to reflect the light from one of the existing light sources off of a small piece of mirror. Strategically placed, several of these pinpoint light sources can add the dramatic impact desired by the designer or yourself. These mirrors can be permanently positioned on a small stick with seal-

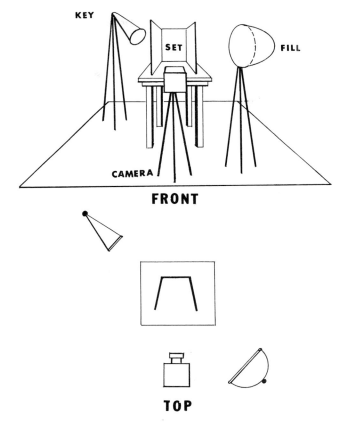

77. *Diagram of lamp position*

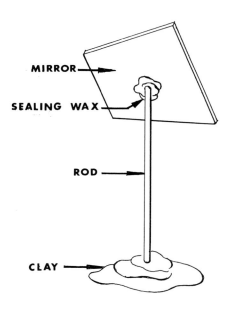

MIRROR

SEALING WAX

ROD

CLAY

ing wax and then mounted to the table with plastic clay (Fig. *78*).

There are several methods by which one can accurately determine the proper exposure for any type of photographic material. The best method requires a very selective spot meter and a good knowledge of Minor White's *Zone System Manual* (Dobbs Ferry, N.Y.: Morgan & Morgan, 1968). According to this method one would read the intensity of light being reflected only from the shadow areas where visible detail is desired in the final print. A second reading is then made from the brightest area of the model where detail is to be seen. The first of these two readings when reduced by 2 f-stops will provide the correct exposure.

Example: If your light meter indicates an exposure of ½ second at f-5.6, you would then close down the aperture of the lens 2 stops to f-11.

The second light meter reading (the one from the brightest area) is then compared with the f-stop and shutter speed used to expose the film. It is imperative that the shutter speeds of the two values being compared are identical.

Location of Meter Reading	Shutter Speed	F-Stop
Exposure for shadow area less 2 stops	½ sec.	11
Exposure indicated for brightest area	½ sec.	64

When compared, the difference is 5 f-stops (16, 22, 32, 45, 64). This value represents the contrast ratio between the shadows and the highlight areas. If the ratio is 5 f-stops, normal development of the film is suggested. If the ratio is 1 stop more or less than 5 f-stops, the development time should be reduced 20 percent or increased 20 percent respectively.

Difference between Highest and Lowest F-Stop Reading	Development Time
4 stops	normal and 20 percent of normal
5 stops	normal
6 stops	normal and 20 percent of normal

There are many times when it is not practical to develop your own film. On these occasions it is recommended that the fill-light position be altered by moving it closer to or further from the model to alter the contrast ratio. In this way a commercial film processor can develop the film normally, and good highlight detail can be retained.

A simpler but not as accurate method to determine proper film exposure is by using an incident light meter. For most amateurs the incident method will give satisfactory results for both color and black-and-white films. Unlike the reflected meter-reading method, the incident meter is pointed toward the camera from the position of the model and measures the amount of light radiated from the lamps. The major disadvantage to this method is the fact that no allowance is made for the particular absorption qualities of the pigments used in painting the model. Thus any exposure determined by this method might be as much as 2 f-stops greater or lower than the one needed to obtain good shadow detail. For this reason it is recommended that the photographer bracket his exposures to compensate for this deficiency.

Example: If your meter indicates an exposure of ½ second at f-8, then expose five separate frames, one at each of the following f-stops while retaining the same shutter speed: 4, 5.6, 8, 11, 16.

A simple test for the contrast ratio can be made by comparing the intensities of the fill and key lights. As in the first method, the comparison should be made between the two different aperture readings when the shutter speeds remain constant. The proper developing time for the film is then as described in the first method illustrated above.

While almost any camera can be used to record the model's image, a 4-by-5-inch view camera with swings and tilts is highly recommended. Without the use of perspective corrections available on a view camera, the vertical lines of the model will keystone when the view axis of the camera is not perpendicular to the model's vertical planes. A similar experience can be observed when the camera is not perpendicular to the horizontal plane. Additionally, the swings and tilts of the lens plane of the camera will afford the photographer greater control over the field desired to be in focus.

Lens usage is normally a subjective choice made by the photographer; depending on the purpose of the photograph almost any lens can do the job. When making record shots of models a 210-mm lens on a 4-by-5-inch camera is normally employed. Compared to other lenses for the same size format, a 210-mm lens is considered a short telephoto. For other camera formats, see the table below.

Format	Lens
35 mm	90 mm
2¼ by 2¼ inches	135 mm or 150 mm

The lenses indicated above will record the model nearly as the mind's eye sees it. Shorter focal length lenses will allow the camera to get closer to the model resulting in seemingly exaggerated relationships between the elements. Longer focal length lenses tend to compress the elements of the model and diminish size relationships.

When a 4-by-5-inch camera is not available and your camera has no perspective controls, the keystoning which results on your negative can be corrected to some degree when the negative is printed.

Some loss in quality should be expected as well as some loss of the negative's original image.

The most common mistake made in photographing both model sets and actual sets being used in production is the point of view. From your discussions with the set designer it will probably become apparent that some sense of dimension is desirable. If the camera angle relative to the stage floor is too low, all sense of depth is lost. On the other hand, if the camera angle is too high then the full impact of the set's elements is lost. For most general and record-type photography, an angle of 20 to 35 degrees, when measured between the plane of the stage floor and a line intersecting the plane of the stage floor from the rear of the set to the camera lens, seems to work best (Fig. 79).

Photographing Model Sets

1. Position the fill light and its diffuser at the camera position.

2. Position the key light behind, above, and to one side of the model.

3. Set the camera at an angle of 20 to 35 degrees to the set.

4. Add additional lights and/or reflectors for dramatic effect.

5. Use a short telephoto lens on the camera.

6. Determine the proper exposure for good shadow detail.

7. Calculate the contrast ratio for film development.

8. If using a 4-by-5-inch camera, set swings and tilts for parallel vertical planes.

9. Set the lens aperture for the amount of field desired in focus.

10. Always use a tripod.

Figure *80* is a typical setup for the photographing of a scenic model. The various elements in the setup are (A) model subject, (B) key light, (C) special sidelight, (D) reflective fill-light board, (E) camera on tripod, (F) mirror. Figure *81* shows the final result of this particular setup.

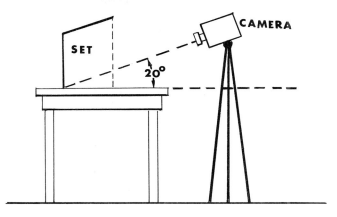

79. *Camera elevation*

80. *Photographic setup*

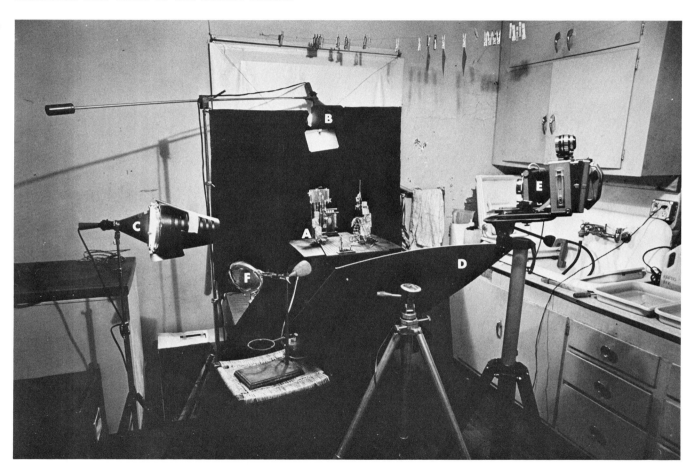

81. *Result of setup:* The
Skin of Our Teeth, *act 1*

An Annotated Bibliography

The purpose of this brief bibliography is not scholarly; what it does present, however, is a small number of books which, it is reasonable to assume, would be in any fair-sized university library and which contain a broad spectrum of approaches to the making of model settings. There are many more books that do contain some models, even giving information as to their construction. Most of these books have not been included here since the instruction they give is too brief or rudimentary; in any case, what they do show will have been covered in the main body of this book. The greatest source of recently completed models will, of course, appear in the various theater journals which appear monthly, bimonthly, or quarterly. Nevertheless, although there are a great number of publications being offered continually, few deal directly with scenic design or individual designers. And even of those only *Theatre Crafts* and *Theatre and Technology* consistently show the current work—including models—of practicing designers. Foreign publications, such as *Tabs, Theater Heute,* and *The Theatre in Poland,* tend to be rich in pictorial materials and sometimes do, but not often, include photographs of models in their articles on production. Most periodical publications dealing with theater can be, as with individual books, found in most university libraries.

The student of scenic design should not, however, limit his attention to theater publications alone; he should also keep well abreast of the developments in related fields of art as well. Not only should he be familiar with those works to be found in single books dealing with individual artists and movements, he should also give his continuing attention to periodical publications such as *Art Forum, Art In America,* and *Craft Horizons,* which help both the artist and public keep up with the ever-changing trends in the various arts and crafts of our period. These publications are especially recommended to the theater designer since they expose and explain new concepts, materials, and techniques which have a direct bearing on the manner in which the scenic work of the modern theater is conceived and realized.

Art and the Stage in the Twentieth Century. Edited by Henning Rischbieter, documented by Wolfgang Storch. Greenwich, Conn.: New York Graphic Society, 1970.

This book which carries a subtitle, *Painters and Sculptors Work for the Theater,* does, indeed, show the work of artists who are not primarily stage designers. The reason it is mentioned here is twofold; first, it does contain twenty-eight models for stage settings, utilizing a wide spectrum of materials and techniques, and second, the work it represents gives the more traditional practice of scene design some highly evocative directions. It should come as no surprise that while the painters included in the book tend toward pictorial and essentially "painterly" settings, the sculptors are more sensitive to the three-dimensional qualities inherent in stage design. For this reason, the sculptors—like Alexander Calder, Fritz Wortuba, and Giacomo Manzu—seem to be more in tune with the designs found in today's theater than do the painters. In fact, the sculptors appear to strive much more to make their work part of the total production than do the painters who, unfortunately, tend to remain their own graphically forceful selves. Nevertheless, this is a book which should be carefully studied by all students of scene design; and while a great deal of its interest is unquestionably historical, much of what is included can suggest to the present-day designer new and innovative approaches to his own work.

Bablet, Denis. *Edward Gordon Craig*. London: Heinemann Educational Books, 1966.

This book, primarily historical in content, contains only five model photographs; they do, however, adequately demonstrate Craig's use of them in his work. These models, and others of Craig's, are definite forerunners for most designers of the twentieth century; in both form and spirit they foreshadow much of the work of Josef Svoboda. (Svoboda, like Craig, often employs bold shadow patterns on massively scaled modular units to define the stage space for a specific scene.) Comparison of Craig's models for *Hamlet* and those of Svoboda demonstrate a strikingly similar approach both in conception and style.

Burian, Jarka. *The Scenography of Josef Svoboda*. Middletown Conn.: Wesleyan University Press, 1971.

Svoboda makes an extensive use of models in his work, especially in the experimental stage. Most of his models are highly finished works, often containing mechanized working parts which correspond to the machinery used in their actual production on the stage. The materials he employs in constructing these models are usually more durable than most model makers use; they are also constructed by artisans who have cabinetmaking skills and sophisticated tools at their disposal. The book contains forty-three photographs of models, although some are multiple views and variations of a single model. This is an extremely valuable book and should be in the permanent library of all designers.

Contemporary Stage Design U.S.A. Edited by Elizabeth Burdick, Peggy C. Hansen, and Brenda Zanger. International Institute of the United States, Inc. Middletown, Conn.: Wesleyan University Press, 1974.

This catalogue contains eighteen models; it provides a good overall view of current design practice in the United States during the first part of the 1970s both in professional as well as in university theater. Most of the models are of the exhibition type and several are reproduced in exceptionally fine color.

Fuerst, Walter René, and Hume, Samuel J. *Twentieth-Century Stage Design*. 2 vols. New York: Dover Publications, 1967.

These two volumes (vol. 1, text, vol. 2, illustrations) were first published by Alfred A. Knopf in 1929. They have, however, been brought out again in an inexpensive paperbook format by the publisher listed above. There are thirty-eight models in volume 2; those shown—in addition to all the other types of work included—are of especial value to the designer studying the varied trends of design during this period, a period which very much forms the basis of our own. This two-volume set provides a good international view of designs from a period which was extremely active and revolutionary in the art of scene design. The relatively small cost of this set recommends it for the designer's personal library.

Hainaux, René. *Stage Design throughout the World since 1935.* New York: Theatre Arts Books, 1957.

This is the first of three books showing a representative collection from a number of countries of designs created since 1935. While the greater number of the works shown are sketches and drawings, thirty-two models showing a wide range of different approaches are included.

————. *Stage Design throughout the World since 1950.* New York: Theatre Arts Books, 1964.

The second in the series shows designs from various countries with Austria, Bulgaria, Canada, Cuba, East Germany, Hungary, India, Israel, Peru, Rumania, Spain, Turkey, USSR, Uruguay, and Venezuela participating for the first time. Again, there are more sketches than models; but the number of models does increase to thirty-eight. There is also a short section in this book, which the first did not contain, that gives the views of designers concerning the use of new materials in their designs along with comments about their particular methods of work and philosophies of production. This information is helpful in showing the trends away from painted pictorial set-tings and toward the more sculptural three-dimensional aspects of present-day design.

————. *Stage Design throughout the World since 1960.* New York: Theatre Arts Book, 1972.

In the third book of this series, the number of models has increased to fifty-eight (which supports the contention made early in the present volume that models are becoming a more popular form of presentation among designers). In addition, the approaches to the construction of the individual models varies much more than in the earlier two books. The various trends which began to manifest themselves in the second of the series become more prominent from 1960 on; designers are using the three-dimensional model to indicate radical spatial arrangements and newer materials which would not be as evident in a flat scenic sketch. The student of design can, from the study of these three books, obtain a fairly accurate overview of the predominate features of scene design as it has developed, as the title of the series indicates, throughout the world during the past forty years. The complete set, although expensive, is recommended as a wise investment for the personal library of all designers.

Kuh, Katharine. *Break-Up.* Greenwich, Conn.: New York Graphic Society, 1965.

In many ways, this book is the student's best introduction to the art of the past century. In it the author quickly traces the most important developments of the twentieth-century approach to all the visual arts, with a minimum amount of verbage. Her commentary relates directly to the problems faced by the present-day scene designer.

Pecktal, Lynn. *Designing and Painting for the Theatre.* New York: Holt, Rinehart, and Winston, 1975.

To date, this is the best book yet available to American students of scene design concerning the technical practices currently used in the professional theater and in the scenic shops—primarily those in New York—which serve this level of theater. Pecktal has also provided a fairly clear picture of the type of work required from the designer working in that particular arena. In studying this book it becomes increasingly clear that model making is a practical necessity for most present-day designers. A number of models, thirty-two in all, are included in the book as well as a three-page outline of materials and techniques employed in model making. Since this book is an extremely valuable collection of specific information, it is highly recommended as an addition to the permanent library of all designers.

Rubin, William S. *Dada and Surrealist Art.* New York: Harry N. Abrams, 1969.

This book deals with an extremely important aspect of twentieth-century art and much of what is pre-

sented has directly influenced all arts of the theater for the past fifty years. This is a work which should be in the permanent library of the scene designer.

Seitz, William C. *The Art of Assemblage.* Museum of Modern Art. Garden City, N.Y.: Doubleday & Company, 1961.

This is an excellent book which traces the historical development of the whole art of assemblage and collage; the text is accompanied by an extensive collection of examples.

Warre, Michael. *Designing and Making Stage Scenery.* London: Studio Vista Ltd.; New York: Reinhold Publishers, Inc., 1966.

This book contains eleven models, mostly by British designers, and has several good color reproductions. The text of this book, however, gives little practical professional information about any phase of design.

Wescher, Herta. *Collage.* Translated by Robert E. Wolf. New York: Harry N. Abrams, 1968.

This book deals less with three-dimensional work while emphasizing the development of the flat assembly of textures, found images, and colors.

Index

111